Using SAS® Web Report Studio for Thin-Client Reporting

Course Notes

Using SAS® Web Report Studio for Thin-Client Reporting Course Notes was developed by Kari Richardson and Eric Rossland. Additional contributions were made by Elizabeth Ceranowski, Helena Pearce, Kathy Kiraly, Mark Stranieri, and Christine Vitron. Editing and production support was provided by the Curriculum Development and Support Department. Hardware support was provided by the Education Information Systems Department.

Using SAS® Web Report Studio for Thin-Client Reporting Course Notes

Book code E70320, course code SBIWRS, prepared date 16Feb07. SBIWRS_004

ISBN 978-1-59994-352-7

Ted Meleky

http://edu/webts1.liveweb.sas.com
Pw= Virtuallab29

Table of Contents

Course Description

This course provides an overview of SAS Web Report Studio. SAS Web Report Studio enables non-technical business users to find, interact with, create, and share reports based on corporate data. You learn how to navigate the SAS Web Report Studio interface and how to build simple and complex reports that surface information from tables, OLAP cubes, and SAS Stored Processes.

To learn more...

A full curriculum of general and statistical instructor-based training is available at any of the Institute's training facilities. Institute instructors can also provide on-site training.

For information on other courses in the curriculum, contact the SAS Education Division at 1-919-531-7321, or send e-mail to training@sas.com. You can also find this information on the Web at support.sas.com/training/ as well as in the Training Course Catalog.

For a list of other SAS books that relate to the topics covered in this Course Notes, USA customers can contact our SAS Publishing Department at 1-800-727-3228 or send e-mail to sasbook@sas.com. Customers outside the USA, please contact your local SAS office.

Also, see the Publications Catalog on the Web at support.sas.com/pubs for a complete list of books and a convenient order form.

Prerequisites

None.

Chapter 1 Introduction to the SAS Intelligence Platform and Case Study

1.1 SAS Intelligence Platform Overview

Objectives

- Define Business Intelligence.
- Identify the multiple tiers of the SAS Intelligence Platform.

3

What Is Business Intelligence?

Business intelligence (BI) uses knowledge management, data warehouse[ing], data mining and business analysis to identify, track and improve key processes and data, as well as identify and monitor trends in corporate, competitor and market performance. – BETTERMANAGEMENT.COM

SAS Business Intelligence includes

- a set of client applications
- SAS server processes
- a centralized metadata management facility.

The SAS Intelligence Platform is enterprise software with components that exist on multiple machines throughout the organization.

4   ...

SAS Intelligence Platform: Architecture

The SAS Intelligence Platform consists of a multiple-tier environment that is typically represented by the following:

- client tier
- Web tier
- server tier
- data tier

5

SAS Intelligence Platform: Client Tier

In the most basic terms, if an application is installed on the machine where the user is sitting, that machine is part of the client tier.

There are three different types of SAS client applications:

- Java applications
- Windows applications
- Web browser applications

6

The SAS Intelligence Platform applications cannot execute SAS code on their own. They have to request code submission and other services from a SAS server.

SAS Intelligence Platform: Web Tier

Java Servlet Container

SAS Web Report Studio

SAS Information Delivery Portal

SAS Stored Process Web Application

J2SE SDK   WebDAV Server

SAS Services Application

Windows UNIX

Web Tier

The Web tier is where the Web applications reside and execute.

The Web tier also contains the infrastructure that supports the execution of the Web browser applications:

- Java Servlet Container (or Java Application Server)
- Java Software Development Kit (SDK)
- WebDAV server
- SAS Services application

7

WebDAV (Web-based Distributed Authoring and Versioning) is a set of extensions to the HTTP protocol that enables users to collaboratively edit and manage files on remote Web servers.

SAS Intelligence Platform: Server Tier

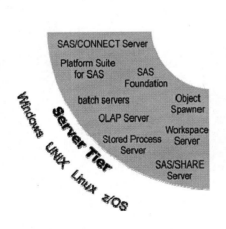

SAS/CONNECT Server

Platform Suite for SAS   SAS Foundation

batch servers   Object Spawner

OLAP Server

Stored Process Server   Workspace Server

SAS/SHARE Server

Windows UNIX Linux z/OS

Server Tier

The server tier consists of one or more machines where the SAS servers are installed and accessed by the business intelligence applications.

There are different types of SAS servers, including the following:

- metadata server
- workspace server
- stored process server
- OLAP server

8

OLAP – Online Analytical Processing

SAS Intelligence Platform: Data Tier

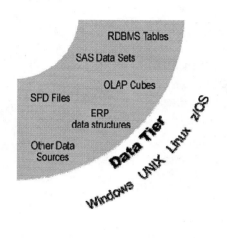

The data tier contains the enterprise data sources:

- SAS data sets
- RDBMS tables
- OLAP cubes
- SAS SPD Server files
- ERP data structures

9

RDBMS – Relational Database Management Systems
SPDS – SAS Scalable Performance Data Server
ERP – Enterprise Resource Planning

SAS Intelligence Platform: Metadata

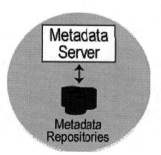

The SAS Intelligence Platform utilizes the metadata server and metadata repositories to manage information about the entire environment including

- server definitions
- data definitions
- users and groups
- security settings
- BI content.

10

1.2 Overview of the Case Study Scenario

Objectives

- Discuss the course data.
- Introduce the case study scenario.

12

Course Data

The data used in this course is from **Orion Star Sports & Outdoors**, a fictitious retail company that sells sports and outdoor products.

- ➤ Orion Star has retail stores in many countries throughout the world.
- ➤ The company sells products in retail stores, through catalog mail orders, and over the Internet.
- ➤ The company utilizes the Orion Star Club to track purchases, enabling analyses of buying patterns and providing a basis for customer relationship management (CRM) activities and targeted product offerings.

13

Orion Star Data – General

The data used in the course from the Orion Star organization consists of the following:

- data ranging from 1998 through 2002
- employee information for the employees located in many countries as well as the United States headquarters
- approximately 5,500 different sports and outdoor products
- approximately 90,000 customers worldwide
- approximately 750,000 orders
- 64 suppliers

14

Orion Star Data – Data Warehouse

A data warehouse was created at Orion Star using SAS Data Integration Studio to do the following:

- extract information from transactional systems
- transform that information
- load it into data warehouse tables

Data warehouse tables were used to create information maps, which are business views of the data. Information maps are used as data sources in many of the SAS Intelligence Platform applications.

15

Orion Star Data – Data Sources for SAS Web Report Studio

The information below are graphical representations of the data sources used in this course.

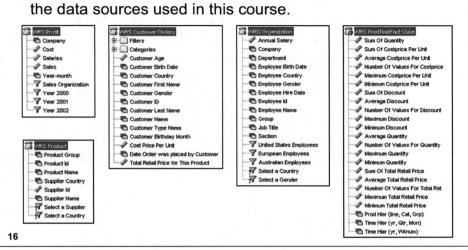

16

1.3 Business Intelligence Information Consumers

Objectives

- Identify the business intelligence information consumers at Orion Star.
- Discuss which tools will be used by the various Orion Star employees.

18

Orion Star Business Intelligence Consumers

Many individuals and groups at Orion Star use SAS software, including the following:

- the information technology department
- business users
- management and C-level executives

19

SAS Intelligence Platform Applications

There are many SAS Intelligence Platform applications, including:

SAS Management Console

SAS Data Integration Studio

SAS OLAP Cube Studio

SAS Enterprise Guide

SAS Add-In for Microsoft Office

SAS Information Map Studio

SAS Web Report Studio

SAS Information Delivery Portal

20

Orion Star Business Intelligence Consumers

IT Department	Business Users	Information Consumers

IT Administrator
- User administration
- Report administration
- Software administration

Data Modeler
- Business view manager
- Understands physical data model
- SQL programmer

Report Administrator
- Report builder
- Schedule reports
- Monitor queue

Application Developer
- Web application builder
- Integrate applications

Business Analyst
- No programming
- Strong Microsoft Excel
- Ad hoc queries
- OLAP
- Publish reports
- Understands business metrics

Power User
- Some programming
- Strong Excel
- Ad hoc queries
- Custom reports
- Modeling
- Analytics
- Understands business domain

C-Level Executives
- Annotation
- E-mail

Middle Management
- Drill down
- Manipulation
- Annotation

Operational Consumers
- Sales
- Marketing
- Customer Service
- Finance
- Tech Support

21

Orion Star Personas – Ahmed

Ahmed
IT Administrator

As the IT administrator, Ahmed's primary job functions are as follows:

- setting user and security access
- performing data administration
- monitoring stability and performance of the system
- supporting the enterprise query and reporting environment

Ahmed is an administrator of the SAS Intelligence Platform with unrestricted access to the metadata. He primarily uses the SAS Management Console.

SAS Management Console

22

Orion Star Personas – Robert

Robert
Report Administrator

As the report administrator, Robert's primary job functions are as follows:

- creating corporate and division reports using business metadata
- using consistent styles and themes for reports
- creating interactive reports that enable filtering, ranking, sorting, and other ways to work with the data

Robert is a user of the SAS Intelligence Platform. He primarily uses SAS Web Report Studio.

SAS Web Report Studio

23

Chapter 2   Introduction to SAS Web Report Studio

2.1   What Is SAS Web Report Studio?

Objectives

- Introduce SAS Web Report Studio.
- Discuss the SAS Report Object Model.
- Discuss business reporting requirements.
- Discuss SAS Web Report Studio user roles.

3

SAS Web Report Studio

SAS Web Report Studio is a reporting application designed for business users who want to view, author, and share reports on the Web.

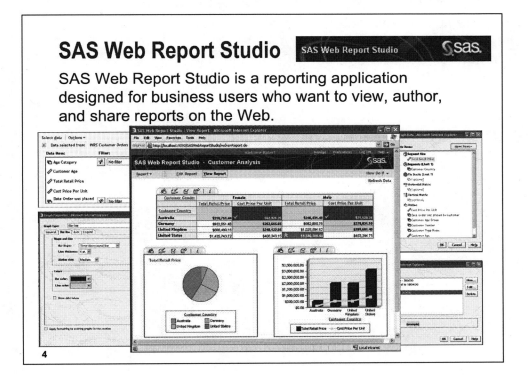

4

SAS Web Report Studio

SAS Web Report Studio reports can contain many different report objects, including the following:

- tables
- graphs
- text boxes
- images
- maps
- stored processes = *SAS programs*

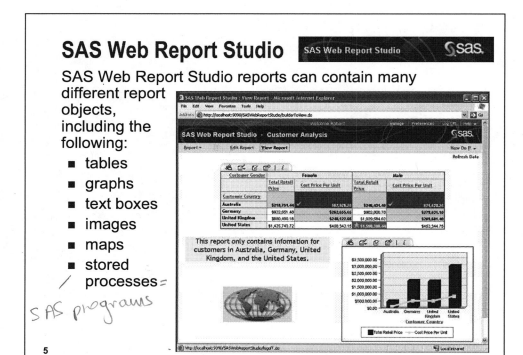

5

SAS Web Report Studio

SAS Web Report Studio is a zero-download Web application, which means that you need only a Web browser on your computer to access all of the functionality of SAS Web Report Studio.

Which Web browsers are supported?
- Internet Explorer 5.5 or newer

6

SAS Report Object Model

SAS Web Report Studio utilizes the SAS Report Object Model format, which stores information about the report in XML.

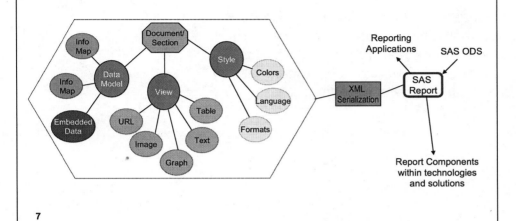

7

Other SAS applications such as SAS Enterprise Guide 4.1 and SAS Add-In for Microsoft Office 2.1 can save reports using the SAS Report Model. Users can view those reports in SAS Web Report Studio.

Business Reporting Requirements

In most organizations, there are many information consumers who need reports from business data, but relatively few people who understand the data structures necessary to build the reports.

Allowing end users access to business data gives them the ability to create reports quickly and make changes as often as needed.

continued...

8

Business Reporting Requirements

As part of the SAS Intelligence Platform, SAS Web Report Studio provides access to enterprise data that is stored in terms the information consumers can understand.

This form of the data is referred to as an *information map*. Information maps incorporate business rules and eliminate the need to understand data relationships. By using information maps, information consumers can concentrate on the analysis and reporting.

9

Business Reporting Made Easy

SAS Web Report Studio enables information consumers to perform the following tasks:

- build their own reports
- receive results rapidly
- change reports quickly
- customize reports repeatedly
- save reports for future use
- share reports with other users

10

SAS Web Report Studio – User Roles

Role	Capabilities
SAS Web Report Studio Report Consumer	Users can view reports and manipulate report data in the View Report view. Users can copy, move, save, rename, or delete reports. Users cannot create new reports.
SAS Web Report Studio Report Author	In addition to the abilities assigned to SAS Web Report Studio Report Consumers, users who have this role can create reports with the report builder or report wizard. Users can also schedule reports.
SAS Web Report Studio Advanced User	In addition to the abilities assigned to SAS Web Report Studio Report Authors, users who have this role can distribute reports. Users cannot create or delete recipient lists that are used for report distribution.

11

continued...

SAS Web Report Studio – User Roles

Role	Capabilities
SAS Web Report Studio Administrator	Users who have this role can perform all tasks that are associated with SAS Web Report Studio, including the ability to create and delete recipient lists that are used for report distribution. This role provides full permissions to SAS Web Report Studio and should be safeguarded accordingly.
SAS Web Report Studio Prohibited	Users who have this role cannot log on to SAS Web Report Studio. Some organizations may apply this role for users who are allowed to access some SAS applications but not SAS Web Report Studio.

12

These roles are established and maintained by the SAS Intelligence Platform Administrator.

Additional Functionality – Help

The Search section in the Help facility allows you to do an advanced search for a particular topic.

13

2.2 Business Reporting Concepts

Objectives

- Understand business reporting concepts.
- Introduce SAS Information Maps.

15

Reporting Concepts

In order to create your own reports and graphs successfully, it is helpful to be familiar with several basic concepts used in business reporting tools such as SAS Web Report Studio.

16

What Is a SAS Information Map?

An *information map* stores instructions on how to access and combine relational data tables or access an OLAP (multidimensional) cube.

> ➤ Information maps can contain instructions for calculating new data items.
> ➤ Multiple predefined filters can be created in an information map.
> ➤ Information maps can contain folders to organize similar data items.

> SAS Information Maps are surfaced as data sources in SAS Web Report Studio.

WRS PROFIT
- Company
- Cost
- Salaries
- Sales
- Year-month
- Year 2001
- Year 2002
- Sales Organization
- Year 2000

...

17

Data Sources

Reports are based on one or more *data sources*. A data source is a collection of data items and filters that describes and provides a view of physical data.

SAS Web Report Studio data sources are based on the following:

- relational tables
- OLAP (multidimensional) cubes

18

Data Items

A *data item* is an item in a data source that is either a logical view of a physical data field or a calculation.

There are three types of data items that can be used in SAS Web Report Studio:

- categories
- measures
- hierarchies

variable = date item

19

Data Items – Category

A data item considered to be a *category* can have these characteristics:

- contain character data (A-Z, a-z,?,*,&,%,$, and so on)
- contain numeric data (digits 0 – 9)
- display data as it is stored in the data source or can use a format to display the data in a different form
- group and summarize measures based on distinct category values

20

Data Items – Category

Examples of a category data item include the following:

- person's name
- person's gender
- country
- department code
- customer number
- product group code

21

Data Items – Measure

A data item considered to be a *measure* can have these characteristics:

- contains numeric data
- is typically used to compute statistics
- has values that can be used in computations or analytical expressions
- display data as it is stored in the data source or can use a format to display the data in a different form

22

Data Items – Measure

Examples of a measure data item include the following:

- a person's salary
- a person's age
- a product's price
- the dollar amount of an order
- the monetary value of an account

A computation based on a measure, often referred to as an *aggregation* or a *summarization*, is based on the values of one or more categorical columns. An example of this is an average salary for a group of departments.

23

Data Items – Hierarchy

A data item considered to be a *hierarchy* can have these characteristics:

- is from a multidimensional data source (OLAP cube)
- is an arrangement of levels of a dimension that are based on parent-child relationships
- provides a navigational path that enables users to drill down to increasing levels of detail
- is used to display summarized measures within drillable levels

24

Data Items – Hierarchy

Here are some examples of a hierarchy data item:

- levels relating to time – year, quarter, month
- levels relating to geography – state, county, city
- levels relating to an organization – company, region, location, department

25

Filters

Many times a report needs to be based on a subset of data to fulfill the analysis requirements.

- ➤ A *filter* is the specification of one or more conditions to subset a data source in order to view the desired information.
- ➤ Filters can be created for one or more data items.
- ➤ Some data sources may also contain predefined filters that can be selected for specific data items.
- ➤ Multiple filters can be combined in a number of ways, providing powerful subset capabilities.

26

2.3 Exploring the SAS Web Report Studio Interface

Objectives

- Introduce the SAS Web Report Studio interface.
- Discuss the functionality available from the Report menu.
- Demonstrate how to use SAS Web Report Studio by logging on and viewing an existing report.

28

SAS Web Report Studio Interface

After you are logged in, SAS Web Report Studio allows for two basic initial tasks: opening an existing report or creating a new report.

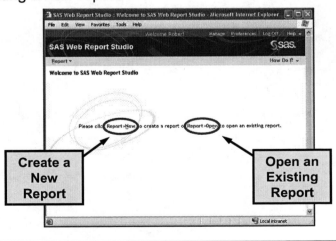

29

SAS Web Report Studio Interface

Also on the initial screen is the Report menu. The Report menu drives the main functionality.

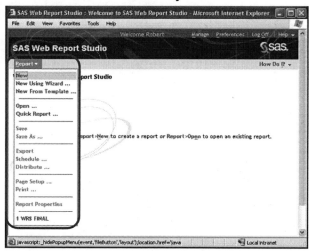

30

SAS Web Report Studio Report Menu

The Report menu drives the main functionality.

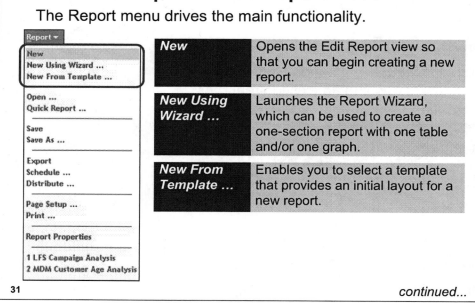

New	Opens the Edit Report view so that you can begin creating a new report.
New Using Wizard ...	Launches the Report Wizard, which can be used to create a one-section report with one table and/or one graph.
New From Template ...	Enables you to select a template that provides an initial layout for a new report.

31

continued...

SAS Web Report Studio Report Menu

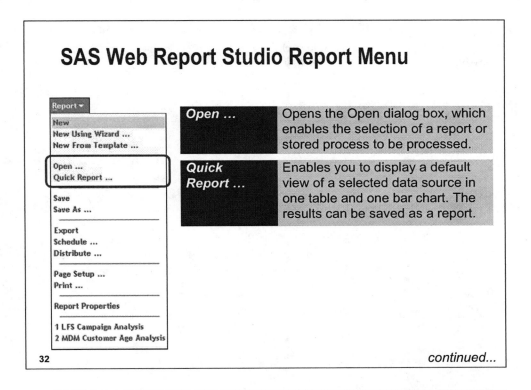

Open ...	Opens the Open dialog box, which enables the selection of a report or stored process to be processed.
Quick Report ...	Enables you to display a default view of a selected data source in one table and one bar chart. The results can be saved as a report.

32

continued...

SAS Web Report Studio Report Menu

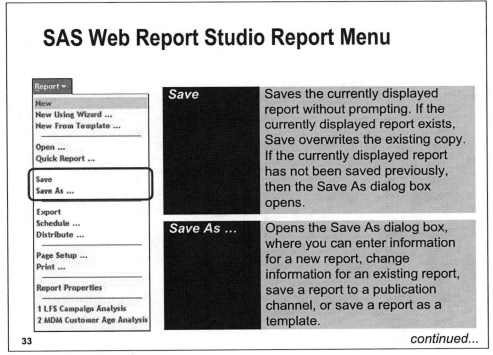

Save	Saves the currently displayed report without prompting. If the currently displayed report exists, Save overwrites the existing copy. If the currently displayed report has not been saved previously, then the Save As dialog box opens.
Save As ...	Opens the Save As dialog box, where you can enter information for a new report, change information for an existing report, save a report to a publication channel, or save a report as a template.

33

continued...

 Publication channels enable you to obtain continually updated information, and to share that information with others. A publication channel is a virtual communication path that is identified with a particular topic, organizational group, user audience, or other category (similar to the way a radio channel is identified with a particular frequency). Your organization defines channels using the SAS Publishing Framework, and your SAS administrator applies security in order to control which users and groups can access the channel.

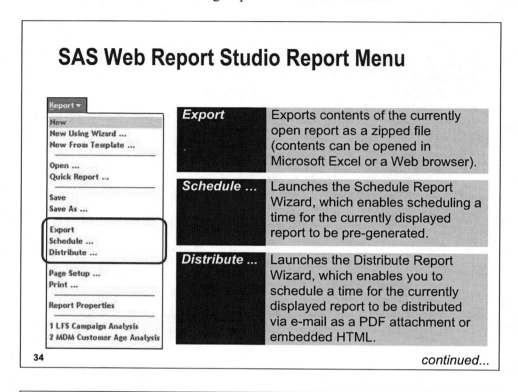

continued...

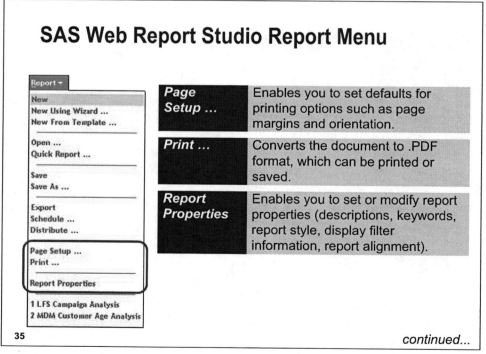

continued...

SAS Web Report Studio Report Menu

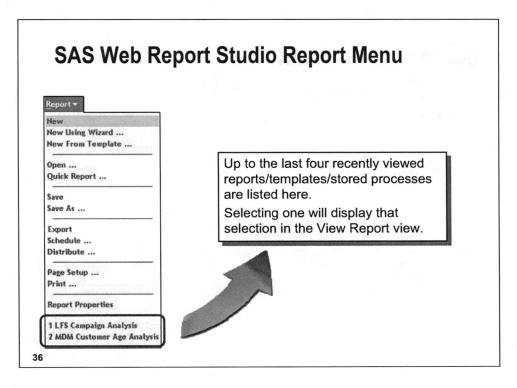

Up to the last four recently viewed reports/templates/stored processes are listed here.

Selecting one will display that selection in the View Report view.

36

Additional Functionality

Other tasks can be selected at the top of the SAS Web Report Studio window.

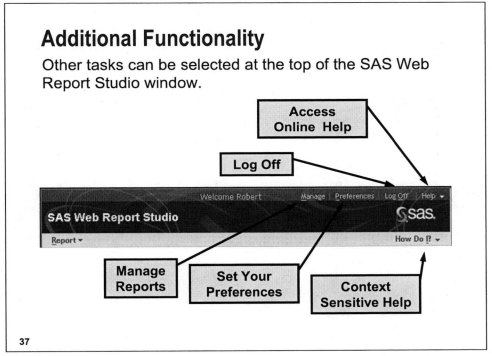

37

Additional Functionality – Manage

The Manage window allows you to do the following tasks:

- search
- edit
- move, copy, delete, and rename
- print
- export
- schedule
- distribute

38

These tasks are discussed further in later chapters.

Additional Functionality – Preferences

In the General tab within the Preferences window, you can choose the default folder used to open and save reports.

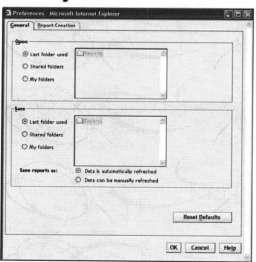

39

continued...

Additional Functionality – Preferences

In the Report
Creation tab, you
can choose the
default settings for
the following items:

- data source
- report style
- header banner
  and text
- footer banner
  and text

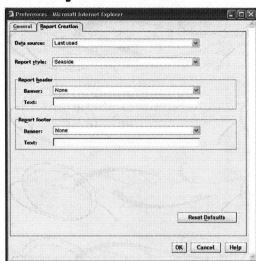

40

Additional Functionality – Help

The Help menu enables you to take the following
actions:

- get more information on
  report topics
- navigate to the Technical
  Support home page
- submit feedback on
  SAS software or services
- navigate to the SAS home
  page
- display information on
  SAS Web Report Studio

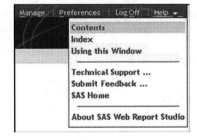

41

continued...

Additional Functionality – Help

The Contents section
in the Help facility
enables you to
navigate through the
Help topics.

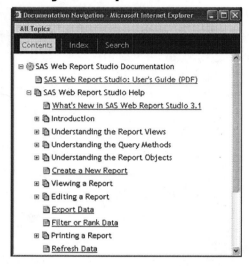

42

continued...

Additional Functionality – Help

The Index section in
the Help facility
displays topics in
alphabetic order.

You can scroll to a
topic or use the
Jump to dialog box to
navigate to a specific
topic.

43

continued...

Additional Functionality – Help

The Search section in the Help facility allows you to do an advanced search for a particular topic.

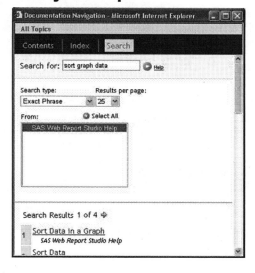

44

Exploring SAS Web Report Studio

Setting Up the Classroom Machine

In the classroom environment your computer runs the multiple tiers of the SAS Intelligence Platform. In order to run the browser applications, you must start some of the middle-tier components.

1. Start the SAS Services Application, which starts some of the SAS Web-tier components.

    a. Select **Start** ⇨ **All Programs** ⇨ **SAS** ⇨ **BIArchitecture** ⇨ **Start SAS Services Application**.

    b. When the Windows command window opens, minimize it by selecting ⊟.

2. Start Tomcat, which is a Java servlet container that allows for the graphical user interface of the SAS browser applications.

    a. Select **Start** ⇨ **All Programs** ⇨ **SAS** ⇨ **BIArchitecture** ⇨ **Start Tomcat**.

    b. When the Windows command window opens, minimize it by selecting ⊟.

    c. It will take a few minutes for Tomcat to load before you can connect to one of the SAS browser applications.

    ✎   Starting these applications is typically done by a Web administrator on a Web server machine and not by individual users.

Logging On to SAS Web Report Studio

1. Start Internet Explorer by selecting **Start** ⇨ **Internet**.

2. Select **Favorites** ⇨ **SAS Web Report Studio** from the menu bar.

   ✎   You can also enter the URL (web address) to access SAS Web Report Studio. This web address would be different at other locations.

   http://localhost:9090/SASWebReportStudio

3. Enter the user name and password provided by your instructor.

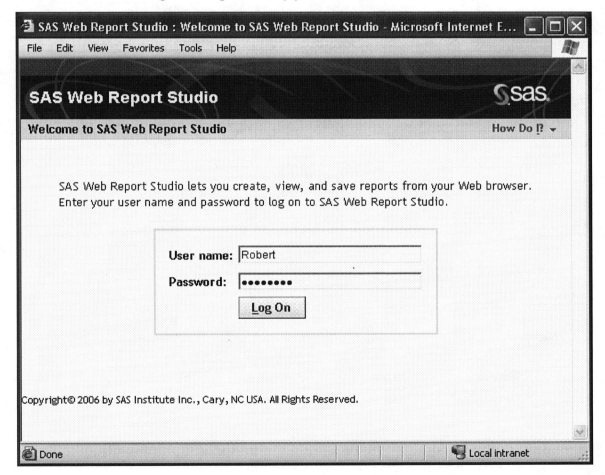

   ✎   The values shown above might be different than those used in class.

4. Select   **Log On** .

Viewing an Existing Report

1. Select **Report** ⇨ **Open ...** to open an existing report.

2. Select **WRS FINAL** to open that report.

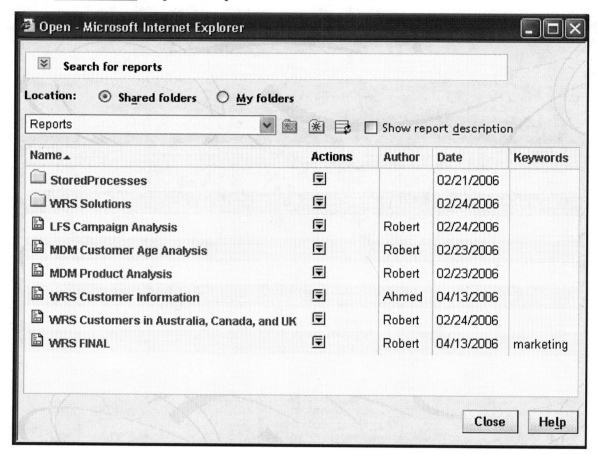

3. The report opens in the View Report view. The selected report has multiple sections that can be accessed by selecting the tabs across the top of the report. The first section contains Sales Analysis information. Use the scroll bars to view both sections of this report.

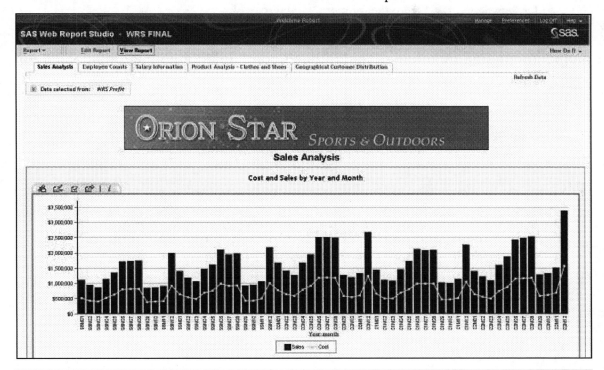

Company Cost and Sales by Year and Month

Company	Orion Australia		Orion Belgium		Orion Denmark		Orion France		Orion Germany		Orion Holland		Orion Italy		Orion Spain		Orion UK		Orion USA	
Year-month	Cost	Sales	Cost	Sales	Cost	Sales	Cost	Sales	Cost	Sales	Cost	Sales	Cost	Sales	Cost	Sales	Cost	Sales	Cost	Sales
98M01	$72,185	$151,066			$13,607	$31,024	$67,664	$147,116	$82,876	$181,353	$30,021	$63,649	$49,586	$108,297	$47,078	$100,365	$50,700	$108,512	$103,951	$225,932
98M02	$63,127	$132,570			$17,043	$39,815	$53,386	$116,048	$77,937	$173,003	$21,214	$46,410	$48,783	$106,416	$33,677	$72,738	$39,280	$87,090	$80,115	$174,600
98M03	$32,945	$71,320			$10,154	$22,525	$46,517	$100,199	$68,975	$150,204	$25,624	$55,802	$40,636	$88,130	$44,886	$94,830	$50,154	$106,629	$82,651	$178,080
98M04	$30,348	$63,855			$14,756	$31,232	$69,932	$148,212	$82,686	$176,305	$38,815	$80,624	$56,706	$121,944	$63,183	$133,375	$60,814	$127,735	$123,109	$259,650
98M05	$29,710	$64,283			$15,982	$34,002	$84,305	$178,441	$93,711	$202,728	$45,237	$94,918	$67,838	$144,134	$75,310	$159,129	$81,260	$172,246	$142,804	$304,483
98M06	$25,643	$54,912			$23,110	$49,557	$106,853	$229,839	$122,019	$261,868	$55,558	$116,840	$86,586	$185,165	$104,954	$223,163	$110,390	$234,425	$170,934	$364,611
98M07	$31,444	$67,506			$16,723	$37,003	$99,221	$207,472	$122,134	$260,461	$50,300	$105,461	$78,415	$168,128	$110,448	$233,364	$113,075	$240,349	$199,410	$420,615
98M08	$25,511	$54,909			$20,242	$42,593	$105,003	$222,626	$122,692	$261,391	$55,658	$116,897	$81,870	$175,475	$106,653	$227,710	$99,478	$213,330	$203,123	$430,906
98M09	$25,319	$54,783			$11,371	$25,416	$48,514	$104,690	$63,967	$138,969	$30,789	$66,076	$37,483	$80,853	$40,388	$84,298	$49,074	$107,124	$89,320	$190,249
98M10	$53,191	$112,217			$9,307	$20,744	$46,862	$101,315	$61,298	$135,000	$25,451	$54,427	$39,539	$86,169	$38,597	$81,539	$44,353	$96,386	$85,352	$183,072
98M11	$53,096	$112,899			$10,236	$23,472	$51,558	$112,119	$63,857	$139,732	$24,962	$53,448	$41,421	$89,128	$42,110	$89,965	$43,465	$95,712	$93,115	$198,565
98M12	$68,085	$144,229			$20,525	$44,303	$114,352	$249,032	$146,442	$318,617	$59,556	$133,461	$99,147	$216,194	$95,328	$202,429	$101,358	$218,325	$218,008	$471,282
99M01	$81,941	$175,264	$15,688	$33,619	$10,754	$23,532	$97,017	$210,444	$97,914	$214,307	$37,379	$80,412	$69,826	$150,733	$47,407	$100,967	$57,760	$123,761	$136,148	$293,688
99M02	$80,405	$171,813	$9,812	$20,887	$15,478	$34,530	$72,935	$159,662	$84,785	$187,257	$32,843	$70,823	$55,529	$121,436	$35,634	$75,958	$48,237	$104,245	$107,388	$234,809
99M03	$34,927	$75,582	$11,649	$25,147	$11,608	$25,183	$63,354	$136,851	$78,599	$170,483	$30,295	$64,218	$55,174	$119,357	$45,066	$94,844	$49,379	$106,737	$114,805	$246,301
99M04	$31,151	$66,280	$22,578	$48,001	$10,750	$23,168	$90,353	$189,759	$112,995	$239,886	$53,181	$110,668	$74,547	$159,029	$61,991	$129,297	$82,003	$171,926	$159,694	$336,434
99M05	$33,794	$71,811	$28,189	$57,989	$14,731	$31,635	$97,111	$205,979	$114,158	$245,627	$48,852	$102,008	$88,025	$186,362	$73,119	$154,808	$86,602	$186,225	$178,189	$380,659
99M06	$32,353	$67,770	$34,532	$73,726	$23,987	$50,734	$130,868	$277,132	$154,731	$329,740	$78,804	$163,416	$112,125	$235,931	$85,492	$182,099	$120,145	$252,622	$226,450	$477,599
99M07	$33,599	$71,170	$28,038	$59,161	$22,210	$46,397	$133,165	$280,300	$141,657	$297,302	$67,069	$137,039	$88,967	$188,436	$84,388	$179,016	$118,383	$249,419	$215,113	$445,293
99M08	$31,382	$65,571	$29,812	$62,522	$20,430	$43,463	$124,482	$264,143	$145,810	$310,844	$69,983	$146,390	$93,886	$199,449	$91,826	$195,971	$108,825	$231,254	$218,913	$461,492
99M09	$27,812	$58,811	$15,208	$32,070	$8,286	$19,645	$58,078	$124,677	$68,917	$148,670	$31,006	$65,634	$41,208	$89,386	$33,278	$70,466	$50,085	$106,722	$99,754	$210,967
99M10	$55,263	$115,468	$11,612	$25,450	$9,922	$22,734	$57,284	$124,512	$59,935	$129,722	$27,193	$58,320	$44,607	$96,377	$32,250	$69,021	$47,469	$104,922	$94,598	$201,804
99M11	$60,545	$128,399	$11,577	$25,094	$11,120	$24,848	$67,337	$145,204	$76,800	$166,687	$32,203	$69,925	$44,867	$96,291	$33,736	$72,010	$47,227	$103,518	$114,255	$244,240
99M12	$69,443	$150,418	$26,180	$57,612	$22,594	$48,702	$152,697	$327,246	$169,384	$366,857	$54,983	$118,018	$94,860	$203,269	$82,327	$174,680	$111,233	$237,606	$235,292	$584,698
00M01	$92,017	$196,227	$18,452	$39,849	$16,053	$35,620	$92,036	$198,826	$124,820	$272,165	$41,787	$89,841	$83,066	$180,165	$56,271	$120,410	$82,002	$178,265	$169,608	$365,198
00M02	$86,872	$184,982	$15,872	$34,017	$15,645	$35,438	$68,917	$150,051	$107,594	$237,239	$33,023	$72,692	$71,435	$157,274	$46,418	$97,460	$70,258	$153,571	$133,898	$292,766

4. Filter the Sales Analysis information to show only the months in 2002.

a. Each report section has a toolbar that allows you to interact with that report section. Select the
    Edit Options icon (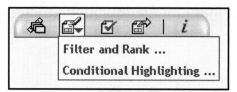) from the toolbar above the graph.

b. Select **Filter and Rank ...**.

c. In the Filter and Rank window, select **Select category values**.

d. Check the box next to each of the 2002 values (**02M01 – 02M12**).

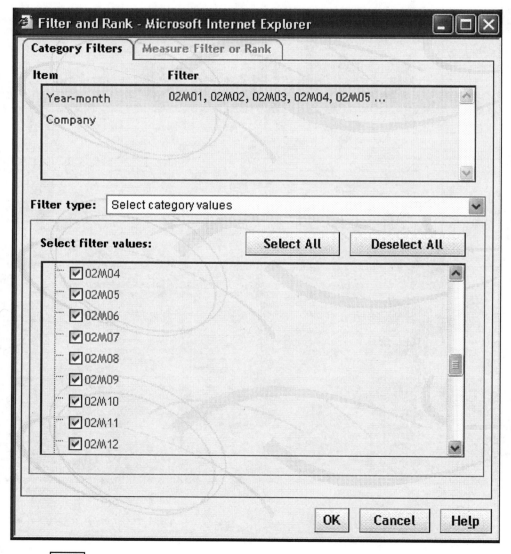

e. Select OK .

f. The report is updated and both the graph and the table now display only the selected Year-Month values. Use the scroll bars to view both sections of this report.

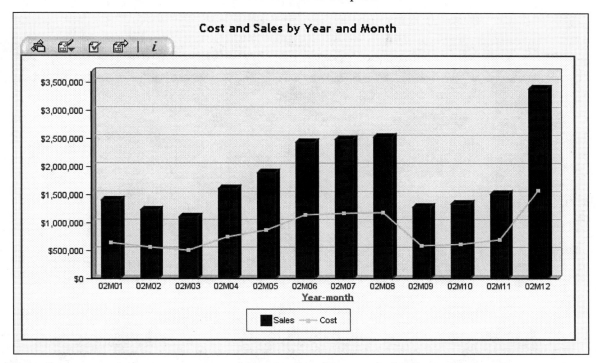

Company	Orion Australia		Orion Belgium		Orion Denmark		Orion France		Orion Germany		Orion Holland		Orion Italy		Orion Spain		Orion UK		Orion USA	
	Cost	Sales	Cost	Sales	Cost	Sales	Cost	Sales	Cost	Sales	Cost	Sales	Cost	Sales	Cost	Sales	Cost	Sales	Cost	Sales
Year-month																				
02M01	$74,771	$159,404	$19,070	$41,180	$14,459	$32,014	$88,154	$191,515	$89,287	$195,802	$41,889	$90,880	$75,585	$163,397	$53,163	$113,441	$66,879	$145,402	$127,969	$276,807
02M02	$69,396	$146,004	$19,617	$41,659	$10,568	$23,456	$78,390	$171,770	$77,257	$168,971	$34,340	$74,483	$76,736	$169,220	$35,929	$76,273	$54,492	$118,265	$108,008	$236,378
02M03	$30,403	$64,236	$16,913	$35,735	$10,508	$22,590	$72,044	$155,046	$75,724	$163,737	$41,182	$87,774	$59,186	$129,498	$45,917	$97,471	$59,543	$127,847	$101,210	$217,247
02M04	$24,577	$52,774	$32,892	$68,578	$15,198	$32,890	$93,433	$198,045	$100,191	$213,325	$68,613	$138,600	$86,833	$187,152	$77,552	$162,565	$89,321	$189,793	$169,646	$356,954
02M05	$37,397	$80,431	$42,737	$91,827	$16,131	$35,109	$101,154	$217,004	$117,877	$252,481	$70,730	$150,122	$120,293	$256,815	$85,735	$182,568	$110,066	$234,994	$179,868	$383,245
02M06	$37,313	$78,477	$51,398	$108,368	$18,812	$41,036	$137,442	$289,530	$162,195	$344,770	$100,329	$211,951	$144,857	$305,602	$128,733	$269,505	$139,331	$297,554	$231,794	$488,856
02M07	$41,680	$89,257	$52,332	$110,008	$18,584	$40,557	$122,376	$257,414	$161,463	$339,716	$96,659	$200,833	$167,819	$353,190	$121,604	$256,685	$151,077	$328,700	$244,222	$512,249
02M08	$35,232	$75,443	$50,914	$106,126	$22,863	$48,433	$133,334	$284,102	$160,401	$342,659	$84,799	$177,728	$165,135	$351,738	$129,013	$273,313	$166,144	$352,648	$243,610	$517,001
02M09	$36,898	$79,060	$20,734	$44,925	$11,039	$24,230	$63,653	$136,141	$80,798	$174,913	$41,676	$89,019	$87,819	$189,276	$59,557	$126,541	$71,088	$152,905	$123,387	$263,649
02M10	$77,705	$163,110	$23,380	$50,821	$13,572	$29,292	$64,435	$138,345	$85,070	$185,081	$41,723	$87,821	$82,061	$179,589	$55,802	$119,179	$61,129	$132,360	$116,742	$250,918
02M11	$87,454	$186,131	$26,682	$57,580	$15,550	$33,655	$71,097	$153,756	$88,241	$192,126	$50,174	$108,323	$95,256	$208,860	$58,971	$124,991	$70,264	$153,282	$135,584	$293,020
02M12	$121,060	$257,931	$53,077	$113,516	$31,554	$69,326	$184,282	$396,451	$214,583	$463,410	$120,292	$257,448	$241,098	$517,646	$132,695	$282,958	$143,995	$305,833	$336,550	$718,532

The gray background around the graph and table indicates that these are synchronized objects. When filtering a synchronized object, the filter is applied to both.

5. Select the **Employee Counts** tab to view the next section of the report.

   a. This section prompts you to select gender values for the report. Verify that both values are in the `Selected Values` list.

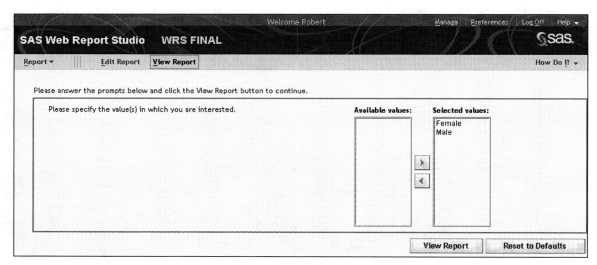

   b. Select the **View Report** button.

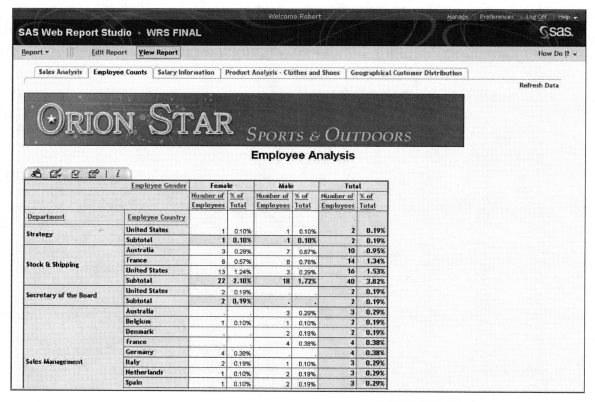

To run the report with a different gender value, select **Refresh Data**.

c. Use the scroll bars to view both sections of this report.

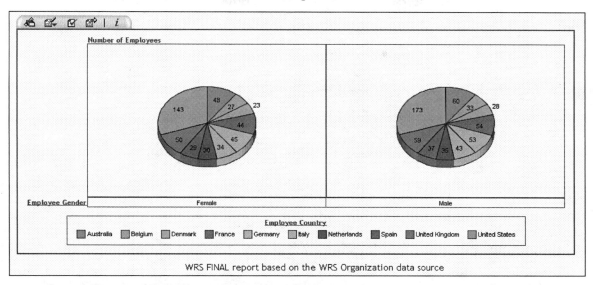

6. Select the **Salary Information** tab to view the next section of the report.

a) To sort the graph by descending **Employee Country**, select **Employee Country** ⇨ **Sort Descending**.

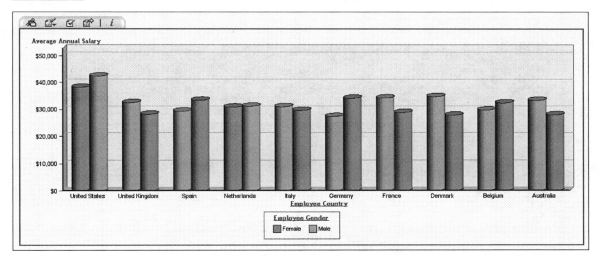

b) Use the scroll bars to view both sections of this report.

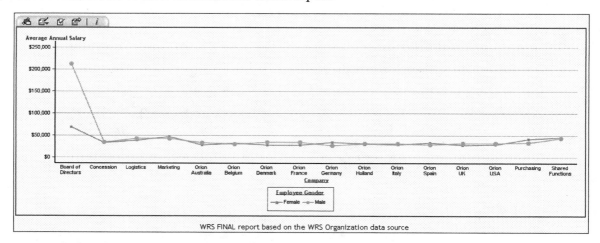

7. Select the **Product Analysis – Clothes and Shoes** tab.

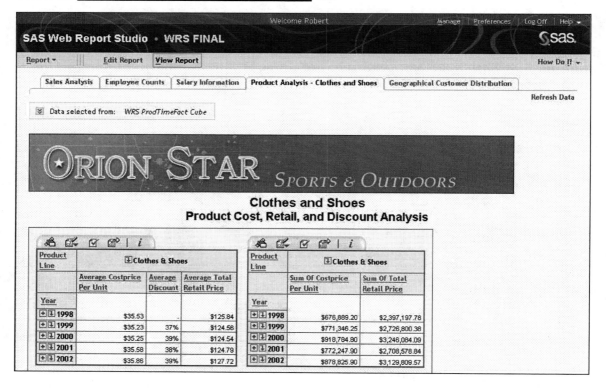

a. This section of the report is based on multidimensional data, or data in an OLAP cube. Select the ⊞ next to 2000 in the first table to expand to the next level of data (Quarter).

Product Line		Clothes & Shoes		
		Average Costprice Per Unit	Average Discount	Average Total Retail Price
Year	Quarter			
⊞⬇ 1998		$35.53	.	$125.84
⊞⬇ 1999		$35.23	37%	$124.56
⊟⬇ 2000	⊞⬇ 2000Q1	$36.06	40%	$92.95
	⊞⬇ 2000Q2	$34.95	31%	$130.28
	⊞⬇ 2000Q3	$35.51	35%	$150.62
	⊞⬇ 2000Q4	$34.53	50%	$122.67
⊞⬇ 2001		$35.58	38%	$124.79
⊞⬇ 2002		$35.86	39%	$127.72

Product Line		Clothes & Shoes	
		Sum Of Costprice Per Unit	Sum Of Total Retail Price
Year	Quarter		
⊞⬇ 1998		$676,889.20	$2,397,197.78
⊞⬇ 1999		$771,346.25	$2,726,800.38
⊟⬇ 2000	⊞⬇ 2000Q1	$224,105.15	$577,595.09
	⊞⬇ 2000Q2	$250,384.05	$933,456.31
	⊞⬇ 2000Q3	$227,204.75	$963,792.54
	⊞⬇ 2000Q4	$217,090.85	$771,240.15
⊞⬇ 2001		$772,247.90	$2,708,578.84
⊞⬇ 2002		$878,825.90	$3,129,809.57

b. Use the scroll bars to view both sections of this report.

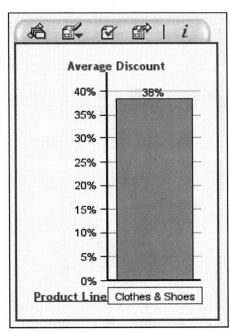

8. Select the **Geographical Customer Distribution** tab. This section of the report is created by running two SAS stored processes and streaming the results back to the report.

    a. This section prompts you to select the values for **Gender** and **Age Group** for the report. Verify that **Gender** is <u>M</u> and the **Age Group** is <u>46-60</u> years.

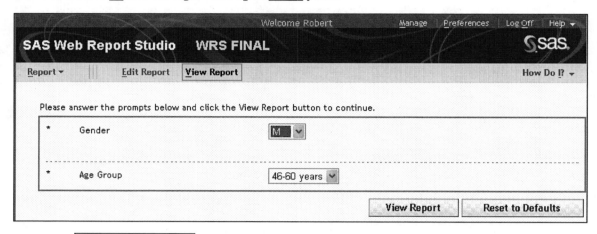

    b. Select the **View Report** button.

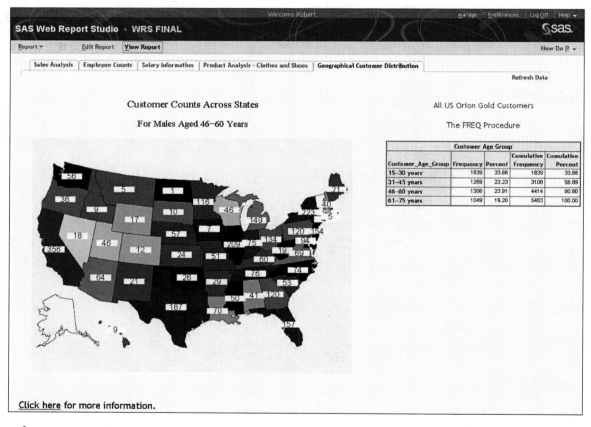

> A Stored Process object contains all the information for executing the underlying stored process code and displaying the results, so there is no toolbar for a stored process object.

9. Select **Log Off** in the upper-right corner.

10. Select [OK] when prompted to log off without saving the changes.

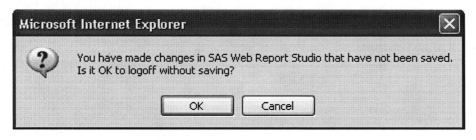

Chapter 3   Creating Basic Reports

3.1 Building a Quick Report

Objectives

- Learn how to build a quick report.

3

What Is a Quick Report?

A *quick report* displays a default view of a selected data source in one crosstabulation table and one bar graph.

The default view is based on three data items from the selected data source. The data items are the first two categories and the first measure in the data source.

In order to display a quick report, the data source must have at least one category and one measure.

4 ...

Building a Quick Report

To build a quick report, select **Quick Report ...** from the
Report menu.

The Select Data Source
window appears, which
enables you to select the
data source to build
the quick report.

5

Building a Quick Report

After selecting a data source, a report is displayed in the
View Report view that consists of a crosstabulation table
and a bar graph of
three data items
from the data
source.

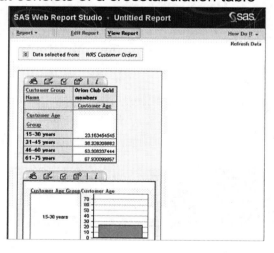

6

Modifying a Quick Report

The initial view of the quick report can be modified. Selecting ☒ in the top-left corner expands the data area, where you can change the selected data items and how they are used in the table.

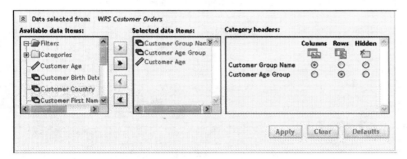

7

Quick Report – Additional Options

Additional options are available when viewing a quick report. These options include the following capabilities:

- edit all aspects of the report
- save the report
- export the report as a zip file
- print the report

8

Creating a Quick Report

1. Start Internet Explorer by selecting **Start** ⇨ **Internet**.

2. Select **Favorites** ⇨ **SAS Web Report Studio** to open SAS Web Report Studio.

3. Enter the user name and password provided by your instructor.

4. Select **Log On** .

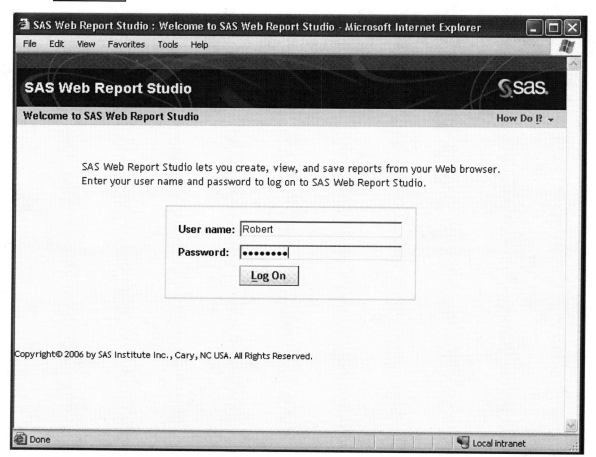

The values shown above may be different from those used in class.

5. Select **Report** ⇨ **Quick Report …**.

6.   Select **WRS Customer Orders** as the Data Source.

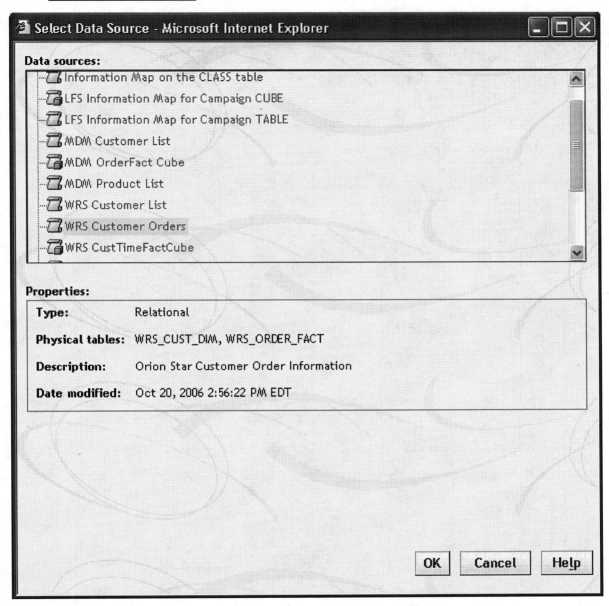

7.   Select OK .

8. After viewing the default report, drag the column borders to resize the report.

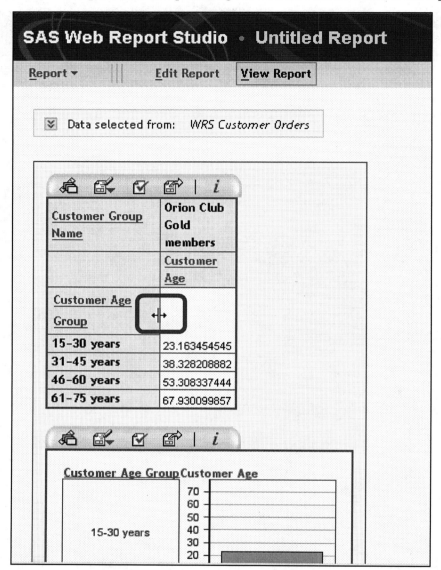

9. Rotate the table by selecting the **Customer Age** data item and the **Rotate Table** option.

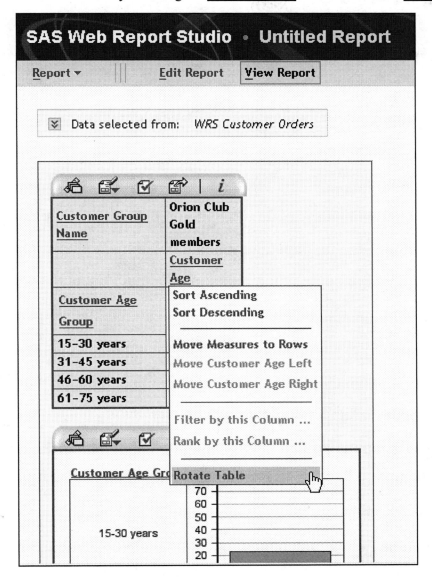

10. Resize the table columns.

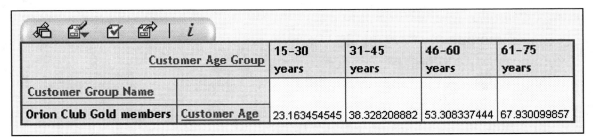

11. Select **Log Off** in the upper-right corner.

12. Do not save the report.

3.2   Using the Report Wizard

Objectives

- Learn how to use the Report Wizard to build a new report.

11

What Is the Report Wizard?

The **Report Wizard** guides you through five steps used to create a one-section report that can contain one table and/or one graph.

The steps of the Report Wizard are used to complete the following tasks:

- select the data source and desired data items
- filter and/or format the data
- group the output of the report
- specify basic information to define the table and graph
- enter information to use as headers and/or footers

12

Using the Report Wizard

To use the Report Wizard, select **New Using Wizard ...** from the Report menu.

The wizard opens to the first step, Select data.

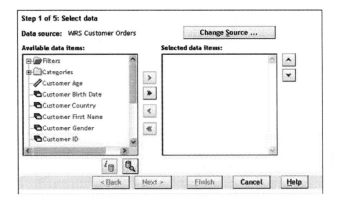

Help is available for each step of the Report Wizard by selecting **Help** .

Report Wizard – Step 1

Step 1 of the Report Wizard enables you to choose the following:

- a data source by selecting **Change Source ...**
- which data items to include in the report
- the order of the data items

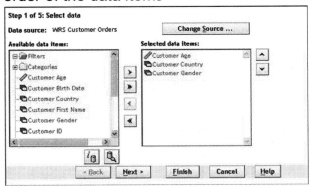

Selecting **Change Source ...** opens the Select Data Source window, which displays the properties about the selected data source.

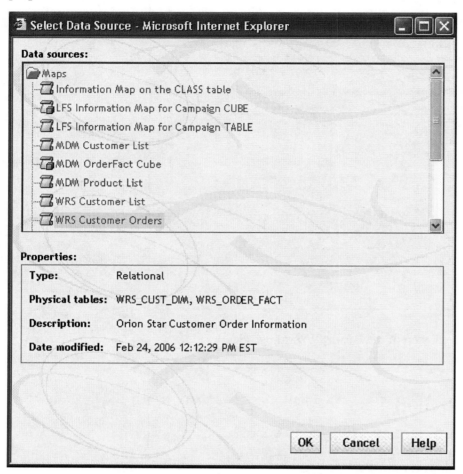

When a data source is selected, the available data items are displayed in the `Available data items` list. To display information for a particular data item, select the data item and then select . The Data Item Information window will display.

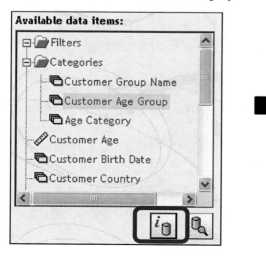
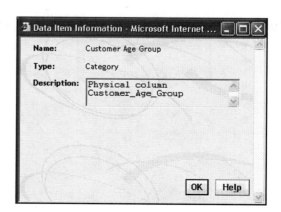

Report Wizard – Step 2

Step 2 of the Report Wizard enables you to perform these tasks:

- select a filter
- create a new filter
- format one or more of the selected data items

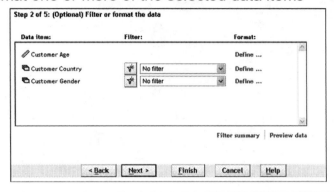

15

🖉   Filters and formats are discussed in the next chapter.

Report Wizard – Step 3

Step 3 of the Report Wizard enables you to perform these tasks:

- create group breaks that will organize the report by the values of one or more category data items
- specify a new page for each new group value
- label each value

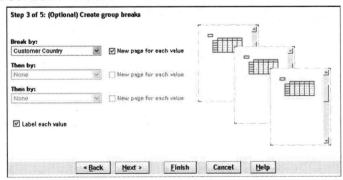

16

🖉   Group breaks are discussed in the next chapter.

Report Wizard – Step 4

Step 4 of the Report Wizard enables you to specify the basic properties that define how the table and graph will be built.

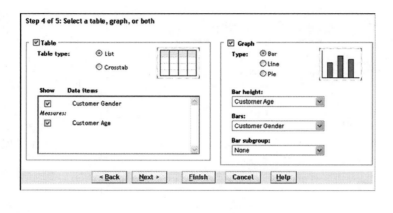

17

By default, the Table section will always be selected, but the Graph section will not. In order to activate the Graph section, the selected data items must contain at least one measure.

Report Wizard – Step 5

Step 5 of the Report Wizard enables you to specify information for the report header and report footer. This information can contain the following items:

- text
- graphical banner images
- the date the query was last refreshed

18

Report Wizard – Edit Report View

Selecting [Finish] in step 5 of the Report Wizard opens the
Edit Report view, which enables you to specify additional
report
properties.

Select
View Report
to open the
View Report
view.

19

Report Wizard – View Report View

The *View Report* view enables you to view and interact
with the report.

20

Using the Report Wizard

1. Start Internet Explorer by selecting **Start** ⇨ **Internet**.

2. Select **Favorites** ⇨ **SAS Web Report Studio** to open SAS Web Report Studio.

3. Enter the user name and password provided by your instructor.

4. Select Log On .

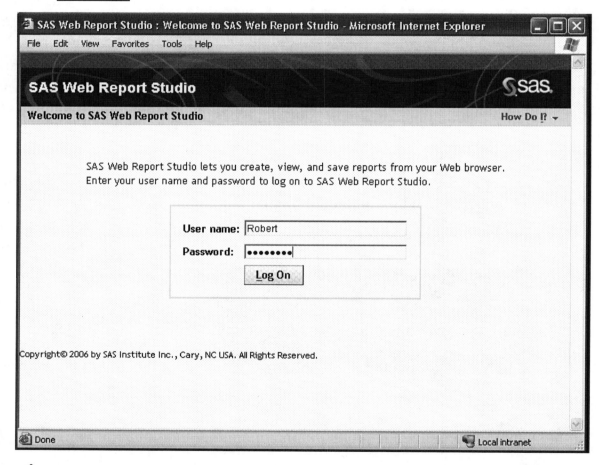

The values shown above may be different from those used in class.

5. Create a new report using the Report Wizard by selecting **Report** ⇨ **New Using Wizard ...**.

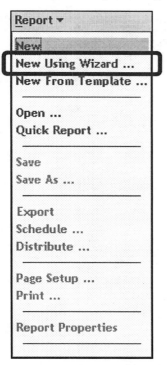

6. When the Report Wizard opens, change the data source by selecting ▮ **Change Source ...** ▮.

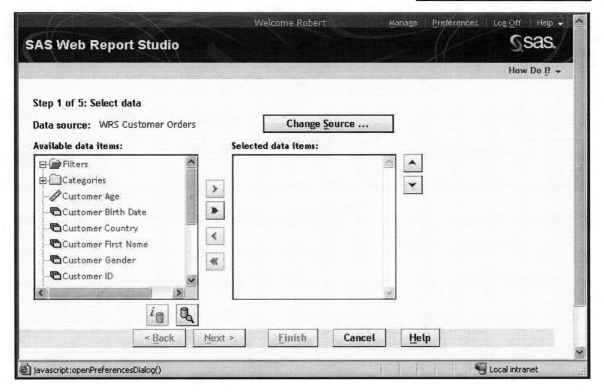

7. Select the **WRS Profit** data source and then OK .

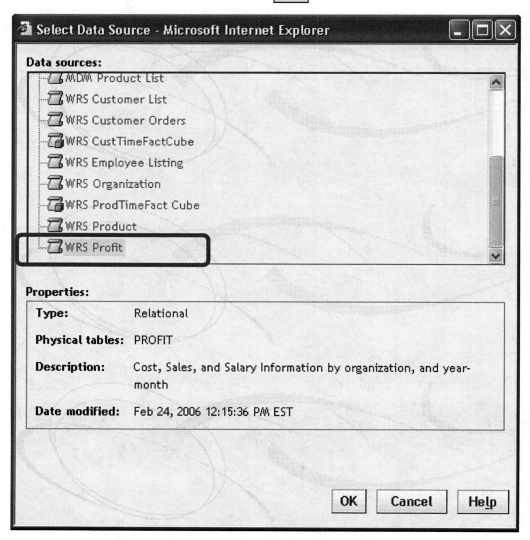

8. Select the following data items by double-clicking the data item name:

- **<u>Company</u>**
- **<u>Cost</u>**
- **<u>Sales</u>**
- **<u>Year-month</u>**.

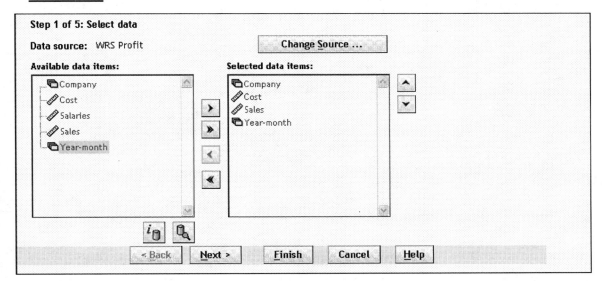

Step 1 of 5: Select data

Data source: WRS Profit

Change Source ...

Available data items:

- Company
- Cost
- Salaries
- Sales
- Year-month

Selected data items:

- Company
- Cost
- Sales
- Year-month

< Back   Next >   Finish   Cancel   Help

✎   You can use ▶ to move the select data items or ⏩ to move all the data from the `Available data items` list to the `Selected data items` list.

✎   You can use ▲ and ▼ to move the selected data items into a different order.

9. Select **Next >** to move to step 2.

10. Because no filters or formats are needed for this report, select [**Next >**] to move to step 3.

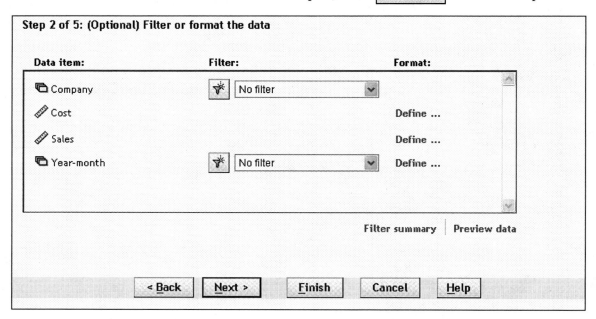

11. Because no group breaks are needed for this report, select [**Next >**] to move to step 4.

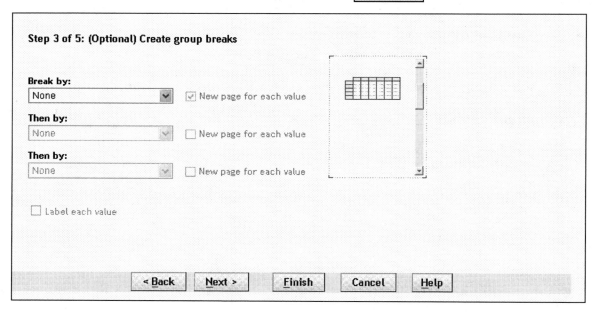

12. Specify the desired properties to create a crosstabular table and a bar graph.

    a.   Select **Crosstab** as the table type.

    b.   Select the **Graph** check box to specify properties for the bar graph.

    c.   Select **Year-month** as the bars.

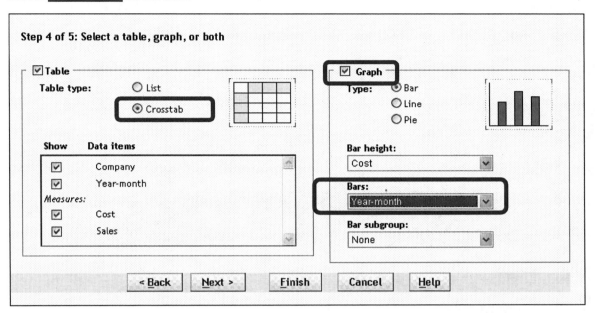

13. Select **Next >** to move to step 5.

14. Specify a graphic image and text to be used as the report header.

    a.   Select **Orion Star Sports and Outdoors – Large** as the banner.

    b.   Enter **Sales Analysis** as the text.

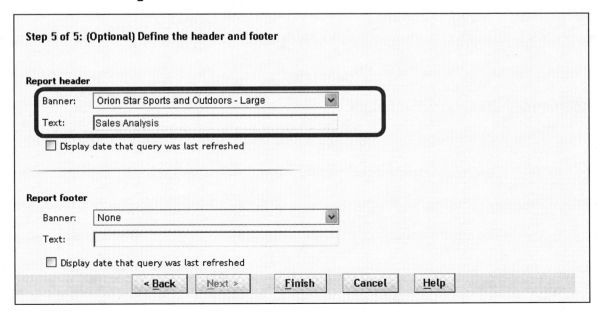

15. Select **Finish** to complete the Report Wizard and open the Edit Report view.

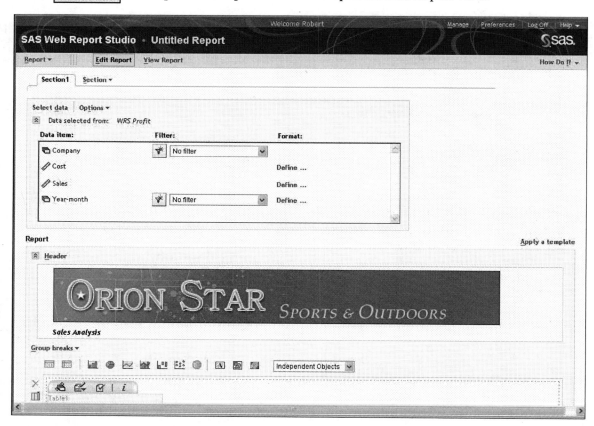

16. Select ❘ **View Report** ❘ from the SAS Web Report Studio menu bar to open the View Report view.

🖉 The Edit Report view and the View Report view are discussed further in the next chapter.

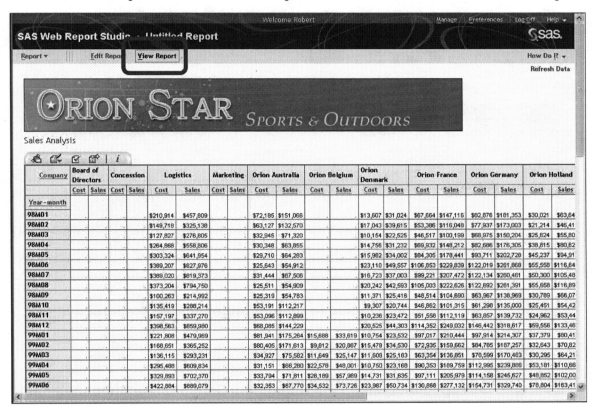

Use the scroll bars to view both parts of the report.

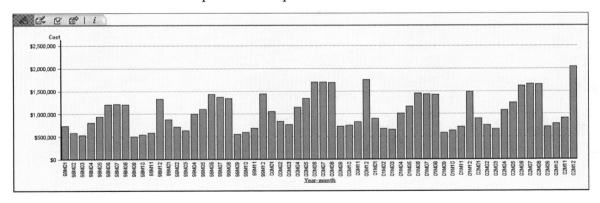

17. Select **Report** ⇨ **Save** to save the new report.

   a. Enter **WRS Management Summary** as the name.

   b. Enter **Report based on data from the Marketing Data Mart** as the description.

   c. Type **marketing** as the value for keywords.

   d. Verify that **Shared folders** is selected in the Save to area.

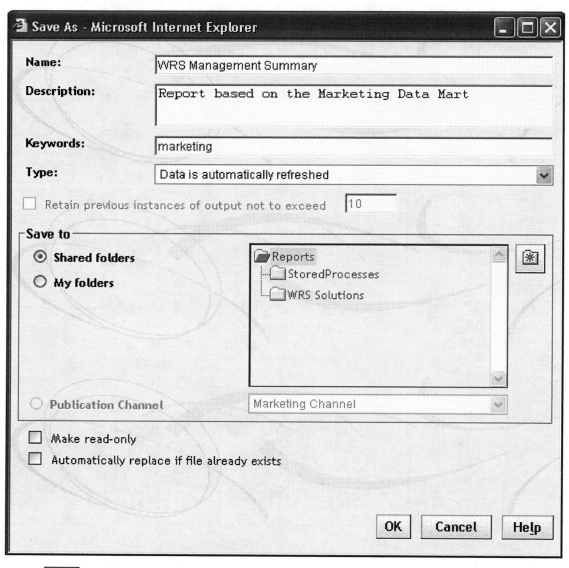

   e. Select OK .

   f. Select **Log Off** in the upper-right corner.

Exercises

1. Creating the WRS Salary Analysis Report

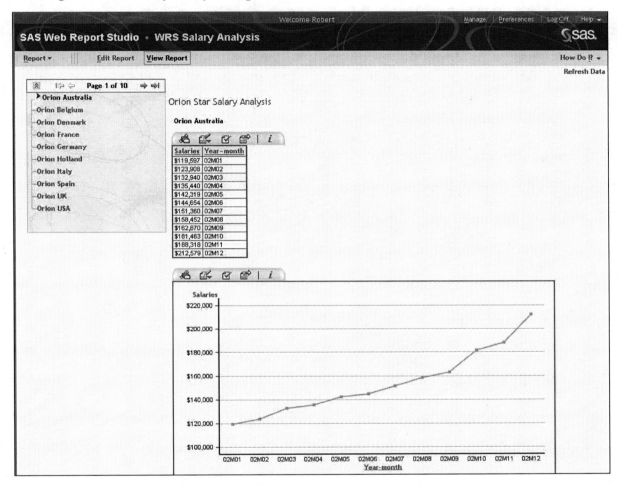

a. Log on to SAS Web Report Studio using the credentials provided by your instructor.

b. Use the Report Wizard to build a new report based on the following criteria:

- Use the **WRS Profit** data source.
- Select the **Company**, **Salaries**, and **Year-month** data items.
- Select the predefined <u>**Sales Organization**</u> filter for company.
- Select the predefined <u>**Year 2002**</u> filter for **Year-month**.
- Use the values for **Company** to create group breaks with each value on a new page.
- Create a list table using all data items.
- Create a line graph using **Salaries** as the measure (vertical axis) and **Year-month** as the line (horizontal axis).
- Enter **Orion Star Salary Analysis** as the header text.
- Enter **Company Confidential** as the footer text.
- View the report.

c. Save the report in the Shared Folders area as **WRS Salary Analysis**.

2. Creating a Report Using Quick Report (Optional)

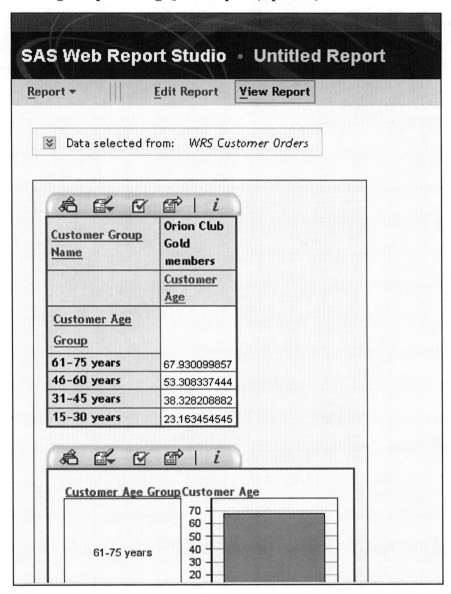

a. Use **WRS Customer Orders** as the data source.

b. After viewing the default report, resize the table columns.

c. Sort the table by selecting the **Customer Age Group** data item and the Sort Descending option.

d. Log off SAS Web Report Studio.

e. Do not save the report.

3.3   What Is the Edit Report View?

Objectives

- Explain the Edit Report view.
- Use the Edit Report view to enhance a report built with the Report Wizard.

24

What Is the Edit Report View?

The Edit Report View contains the section menu, data area, and Report area to create new reports or edit existing reports.

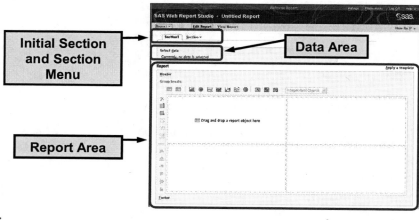

25

Edit Report View – Data Area

The data area of the Edit Report view is used to perform the following tasks:

- select data sources
- select data items to appear in the report
- select predefined filters or create new filters
- create new data items
- define formatting
- preview data

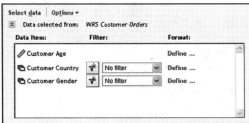

26

After the data has been selected, the Data area can be collapsed by selecting ⊼ . This provides more room when working with the Report area. Select ⊻ to expand the Data area.

Edit Report View – Report Area

The Report area of the Edit Report view is used to insert, position, and set properties on report objects such as graphs, tables, text, and images within the Report grid.

You can also set group breaks and specify header and footer information.

Report Grid

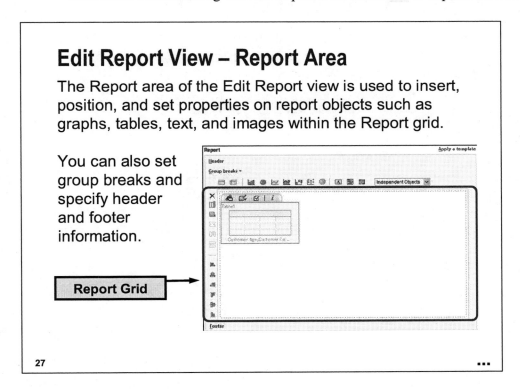

27

The Report grid is discussed in more detail in Chapter 4.

Edit Report View – Section Menu

The Section menu of the Edit Report view is used to interact with the various report sections.

If a report has multiple sections, a tab will appear at the top of the report for each section. Selecting a tab will enable you build or edit that section.

The Section menu provides the following capabilities:
- add new sections
- rename existing sections
- reorder the sections
- delete sections

28

Edit Report View and View Report View

Toggling between the Edit Report view and the View Report view enables you to change the report properties and see how those changes look before saving your final report.

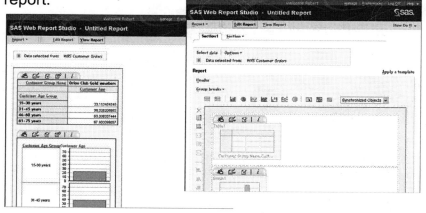

29

Using the Edit Report View

Modify the WRS Management Summary report created in the previous demonstration.

- Filter the data to report only on the Orion Star sales organization.
- Move the graph above the table.
- Add a title to both the graph and the table.
- Change the font, color, and size of the report header.

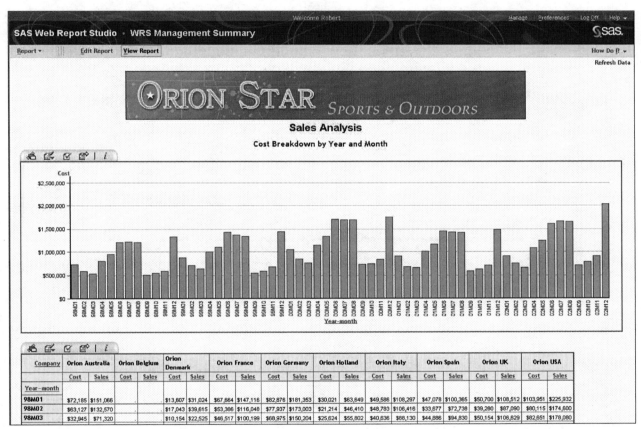

1. If necessary, open a browser window, select **Favorites** ⇨ **SAS Web Report Studio**, enter the user name and password provided by your instructor, and select **Log On** .

 SAS Web Report Studio will time out when it has not been used for a specific amount of time (30 minutes by default). When SAS Web Report Studio times out, you will be prompted to re-enter your credentials before you can continue working.

2. Open the WRS Management Summary report.

   a. Select **Report** ⇨ **Open ...**.

   b. Select the **WRS Management Summary** report by clicking on the report name to open the report in the View Report view.

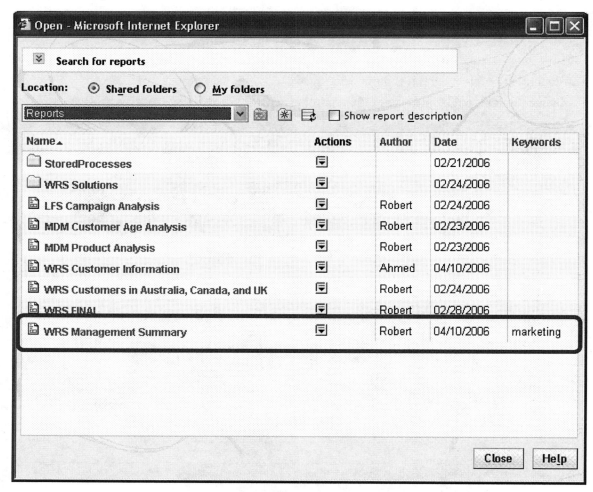

3. Switch to the Edit Report view by selecting **Edit Report** on the SAS Web Report Studio menu bar.

4. Filter the data to report on the Orion Star sales organization only, then collapse the data area.

a. In the Data area, select the predefined **Sales Organization** filter from the Filter column for the **Company** data item.

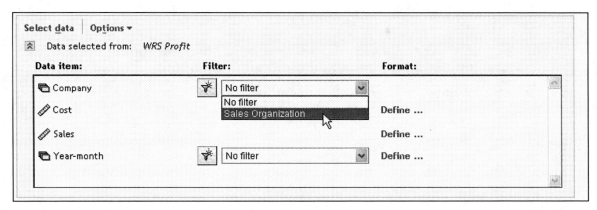

b. Select ⊼ to collapse the data area.

5. Move the graph above the table.

a. In the Report grid, select the **Graph1** object and drag it on top of the Table1 object.

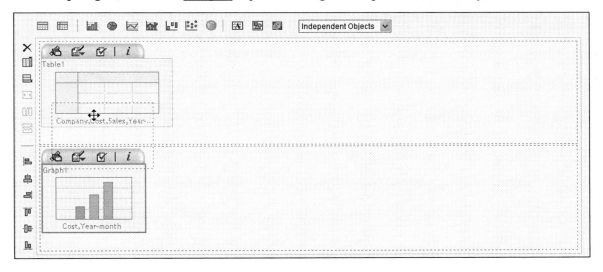

The following dialog window opens:

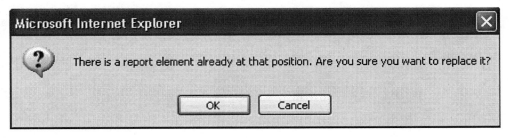

b. Select OK to position the graph above the table.

6. Add a title to the graph.

    a. Locate the object labeled Graph1 in the Report grid.

    b. Select the Graph properties tool (☑) from the Graph1 toolbar to open the Graph Properties window.

    c. On the General tab, enter **Cost Breakdown by Year and Month** as the title text.

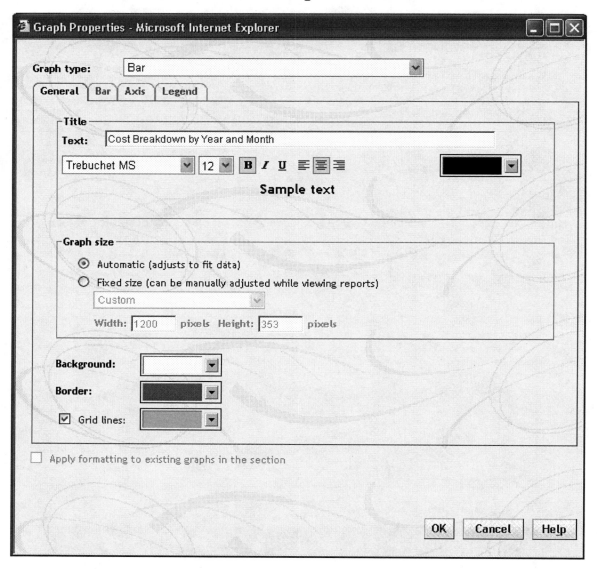

✎   The Graph properties window is discussed further in the next chapter.

    d. Select **OK** to close the Graph Properties window.

7. Add a title to the table.

    a. Locate the object labeled Table1 in the Report grid.

    b. Select the Table properties tool (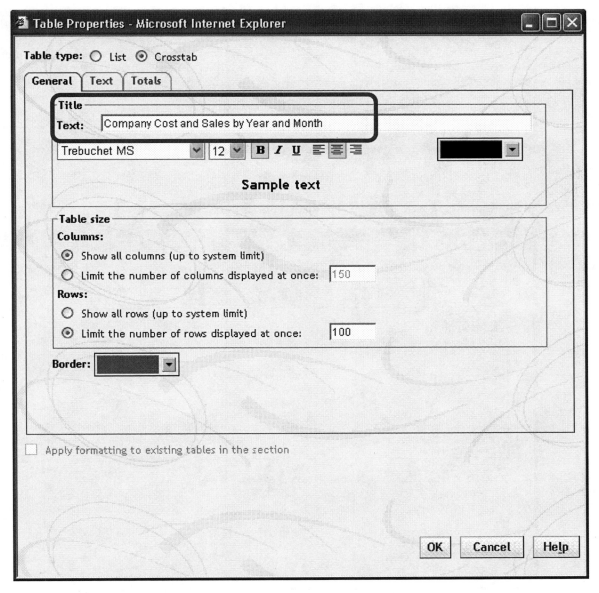) from the Table1 toolbar to open the Table properties window.

    c. On the Table tab, enter **Company Cost and Sales by Year and Month** as the title text.

The Table properties window is discussed in the next chapter.

d. Select **OK** and the Report grid is updated to show the changes.

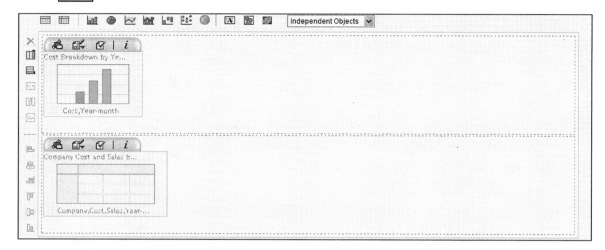

✎   The Report grid does not show all of the detail for the objects it contains.

8. Change the font, color, and size of the report header.

a. In the Report area, select **Header** to display the Edit Header window.

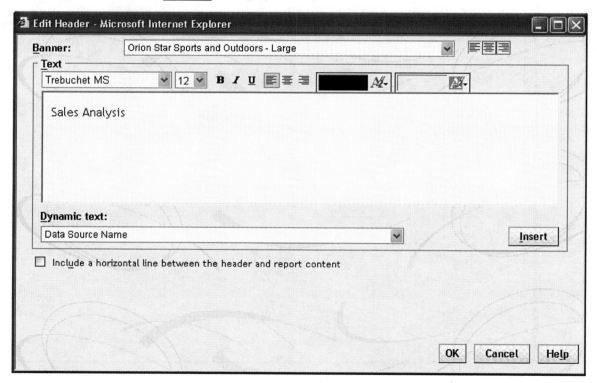

b. In the Banner area, select the center button (⧉) to center the banner image.

c. Specify attributes of the title text in the Text area as follows:

1) Select the header text (Sales Analysis) by clicking and dragging the mouse over the text.

2) Select the first drop-down box and select **Arial**.

3) Select the second drop-down box and select **16 pt**.

4) Select the bold button (**B**).

5) Select the center button (≣).

6) Select the text foreground color box (▮ A̲) and choose a blue shade of your choice.

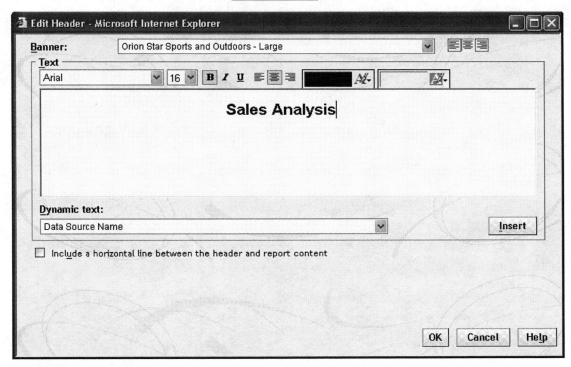

d. Select OK to exit the Edit Header window.

9. Select **View Report** from the SAS Web Report Studio menu bar to toggle to View Report view to see the changes.

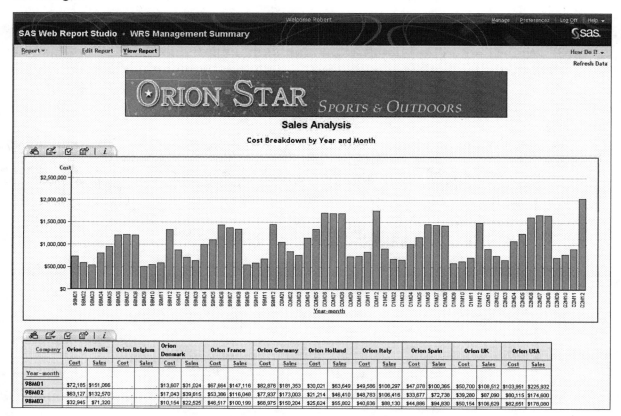

10. Save the report by selecting **Report** ⇨ **Save**.

11. Select **Log Off** in the upper-right corner.

Exercises

3. Modifying the WRS Salary Analysis Report

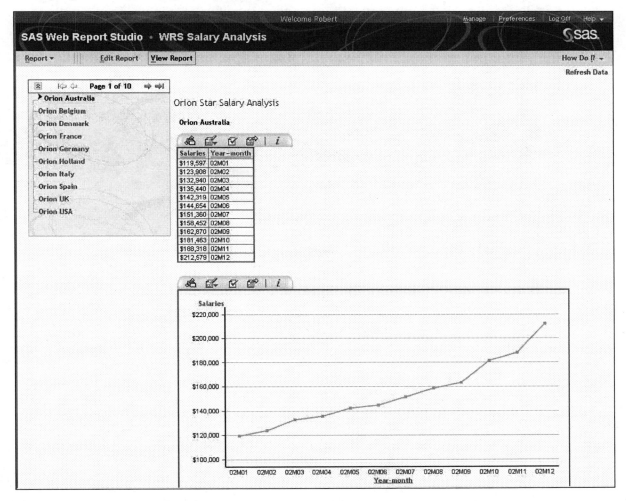

a. Log on to SAS Web Report Studio using the credentials provided by your instructor.

b. Open the WRS Salary Analysis Report.

c. Use the Edit Report view to modify the report based on the following criteria and then view the report:

   1) Modify the report header and footer to use fonts, colors, and other attributes of your choice. (Hint: Highlight the text before changing attributes.)

   2) Use the Line tab of the Graph Properties window to change the thickness of the line.

d. Save the report, replacing the previous version.

e. Log off of SAS Web Report Studio.

3.4 Solutions to Exercises

1. **Creating the WRS Salary Analysis Report**

   a. Log on to SAS Web Report Studio using the credentials provided by your instructor.

   1) Start Internet Explorer by selecting **Start** ⇨ **Internet**.

   2) Select **Favorites** ⇨ **SAS Web Report Studio**.

   3) Enter the user name and password provided by your instructor.

   4) Select **Log On**.

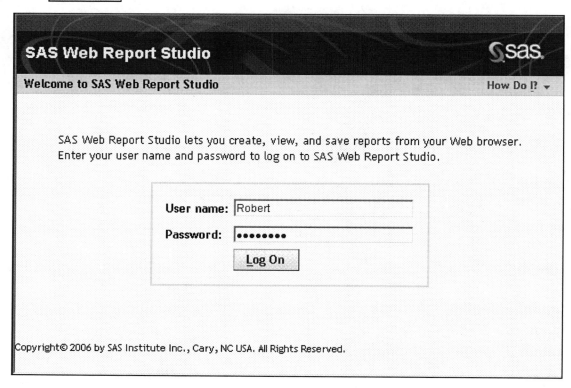

b. Use the Report Wizard to build a new report.

1) Select **Report** ⇨ **New Using Wizard…**.

2) Select [**Change Source …**] ⇨ **WRS Profit** ⇨ [OK].

3) Double-click **Company**, **Salaries**, and **Year-month** to move them to the `Selected data items` pane.

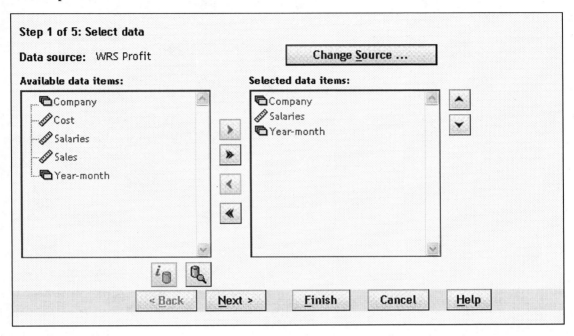

4) Select [**Next >**].

5) In the Filter column, select **Sales Organization** from the drop-down list for **Company** and **Year 2002** from the drop-down list for **Year-month**.

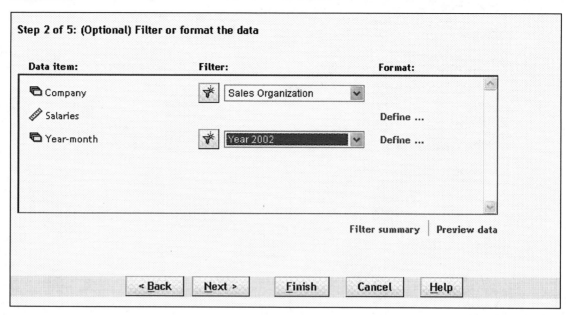

6) Select **Next >** .

7) Select **Company** in the drop-down list for **Break by** and select **New page for each value**.

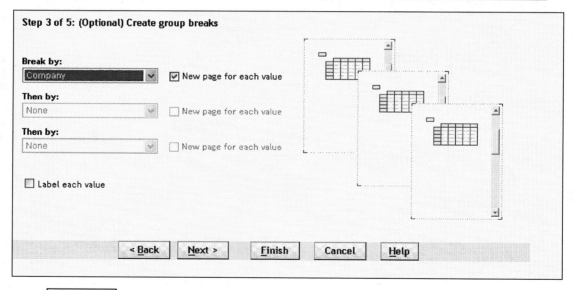

8) Select **Next >** .

9) Accept the defaults in the table section. Select the **Graph** check box and select **Line** as the type.

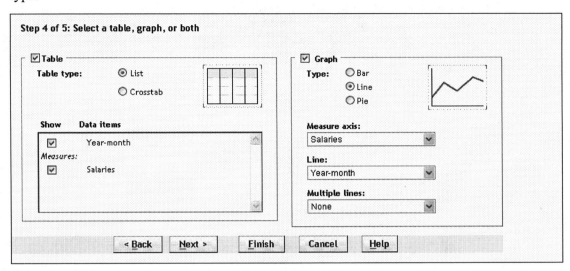

10) Select **Next >**.

11) Type **Orion Star Salary Analysis** as the text for the Report header and **Company Confidential** as the text for the Report footer.

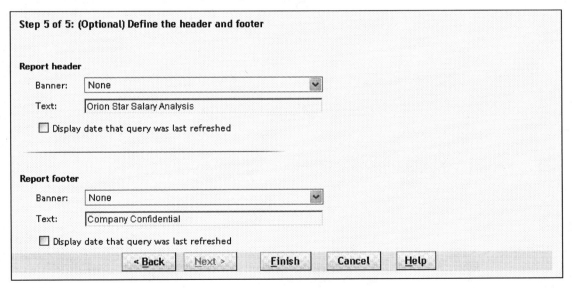

12) Select **Finish**.

13) Select **View Report**.

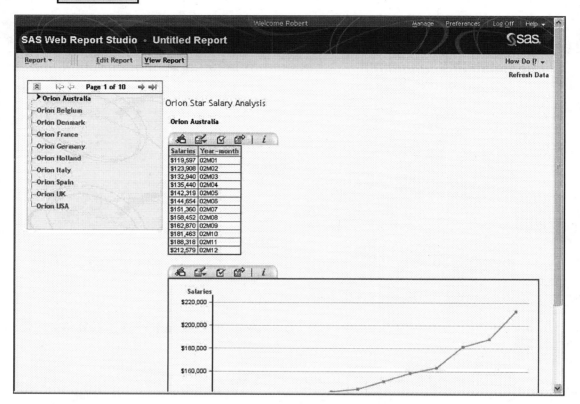

✎   The table in the upper-left corner is used to navigate to the various pages of output. Selecting a company name will display the page of the report.

c. Save the report in the Shared folders area as **WRS Salary Analysis**.

1) Select **Report** ⇨ **Save As ...**.

2) Enter **WRS Salary Analysis** as the name.

3) Verify that **Shared Folders** is selected in the Save to area.

4) Select OK .

2. Creating a Report Using Quick Report (Optional)

a. Open Quick Report and use the **WRS Customer Orders** data source.

    1) Select **Report** ⇨ **Quick Report...**

    2) Select the **WRS Customer Orders** data source.

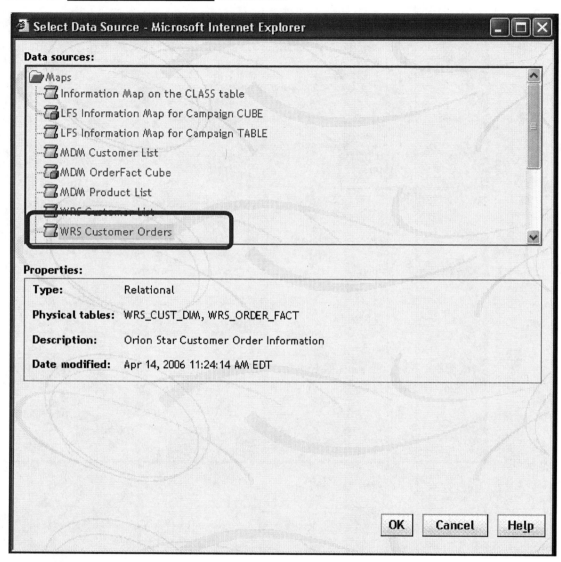

    3) Select **OK** to close the Select Data Source window.

b. The report displays with the default view. Resize the columns in the table by selecting and dragging the column borders.

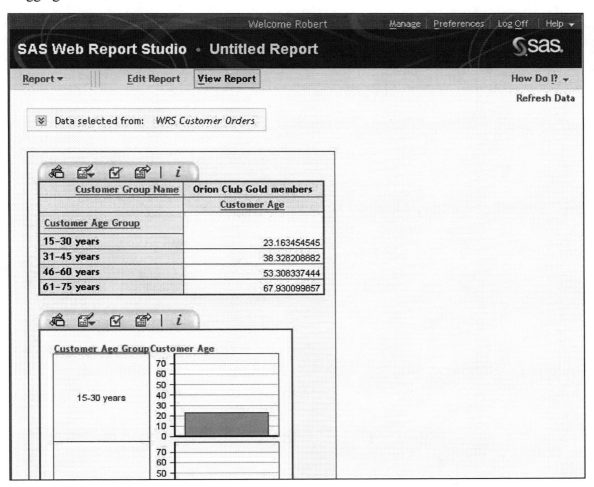

c. Sort the table by selecting **Customer Age Group** ⇨ **Sort Descending**.

d. Select Log Off .

e. Do not save the report.

3. **Modifying the WRS Salary Analysis Report**

    a. Log on to SAS Web Report Studio using the credentials provided by your instructor.

      1) Start Internet Explorer by selecting **Start** ⇨ **Internet**.

      2) Select **Favorites** ⇨ **SAS Web Report Studio**.

      3) Enter the user name and password provided by your instructor and select Log On .

    b. Use the Edit Report view to modify the report.

      1) Select **Report** ⇨ **Open…** ⇨ **WRS Salary Analysis**.

        a) Select Edit Report to toggle to the Edit Report view.

        b) Modify the report header and footer to use fonts, colors, and other attributes of your choice.

        c) Select Header .

        d) In the Text section, select the header text (Orion Star Salary Analysis) by clicking and dragging the mouse over the text.

        e) Edit attributes of your choice; the example below uses the Arial font in a 16 pt. size, is centered, and has a blue foreground text color.

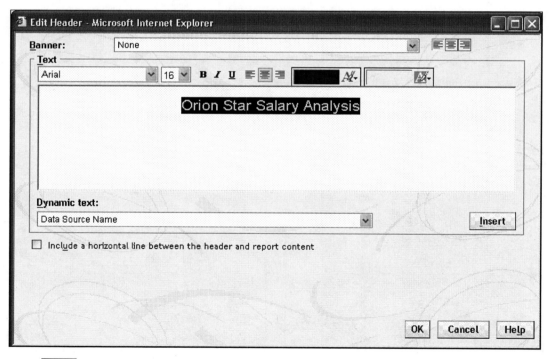

        f) Select OK to exit the Edit Header window.

g) Select | Footer | in the Report area.

h) In the Text section, select the footer text (Company Confidential) by clicking and dragging the mouse over the text.

i) Edit attributes of your choice; the example below uses the Arial font in a 10 pt. size and is centered.

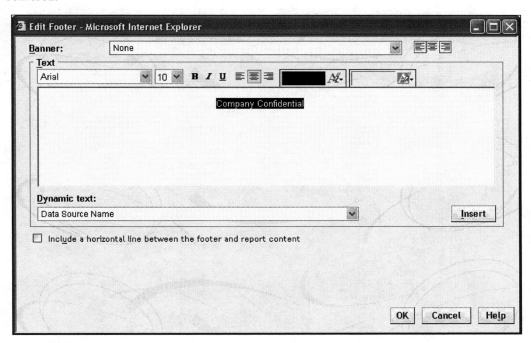

j) Select | OK | to exit the Edit Footer window.

2) Use the Line tab of the Graph Properties window to change the thickness of the line.

a) Locate the object labeled Graph1 in the Report grid.

b) Select the Graph properties button (☑) from the Graph1 toolbar to open the Graph Properties window.

c) Select the **Line** tab.

d) Select a line thickness value of your choice; the example below uses **4 pt**.

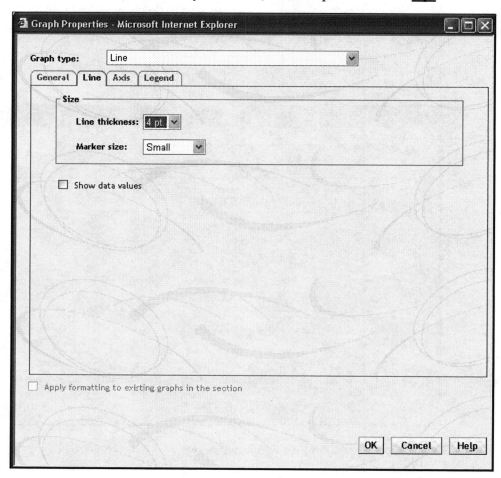

e) Select OK to close the Graph Properties window.

f) Select **View Report** to view the changes to the report.

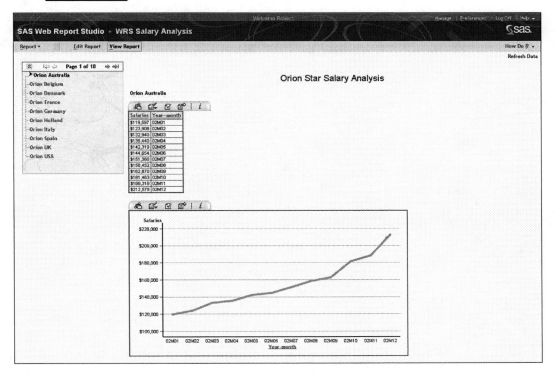

c. Save the report, replacing the previous version by selecting **Report** ⇨ **Save**.

d. Select **Log Off** in the upper-right corner.

Chapter 4   Creating Reports Using the Edit Report View

4.1 Understanding Report Objects

Objectives

- Review the elements of the Edit Report view.
- Introduce the SAS Web Report Studio report objects and the properties for each.
- Create a new report using the Edit Report view.

3

Edit Report View – Report Area (Review)

The Report area of the Edit Report view is used to insert, position, and set properties on report objects such as graphs, tables, text, and images within the Report grid.

You can also set group breaks and specify header and footer information.

Report Grid

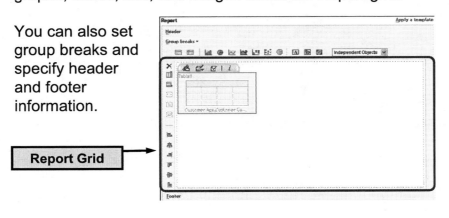

4

Report Objects

Each section in a SAS Web Report Studio report can contain multiple report objects:

- list
- crosstab
- bar chart
- pie chart
- line graph
- bar-line chart
- progressive bar chart
- scatter plot
- geographical map
- text
- image
- stored process

5

Report Objects – List

A list table is a two-dimensional representation of data in which the data values are arranged in unlabeled rows and labeled columns.

Customer Id	Customer Name	Customer Country	Customer Gender	Customer Age
51908	Adam Matheson	United States	Male	43
52929	Adam Moorhouse	United States	Male	28
12718	Adam Selaya	United States	Male	63
7314	Adam Tercioglo	United States	Male	54
28213	Adam Vavricka	United States	Male	53
44308	Adamis Muyamuna	United States	Male	63
34320	Adamo Revolon	Italy	Male	38
74178	Addolorato Girino	Italy	Male	44
59201	Adel Tessener	United States	Male	53
47198	Adela Arenas Vidal	Spain	Female	28
45898	Adelaide Guilbert	France	Female	54
39017	Adele Emmett	United Kingdom	Female	34
43653	Adele Stankhome	United Kingdom	Male	53
60101	Adeleaka Bilder	United States	Female	44
41971	Adelene Archibold	Australia	Female	38

Rows 106 - 120

6

List – Table Data

The Table Data window for a List object provides the mechanism to select the following:

- data items that populate the columns of the list table
- hidden data items

7

List – Table Properties

The General tab in the Table Properties window for a list object allows you to select the following:

- title text, font style, size, color, and alignment
- number of columns and rows to display
- border color
- formatting

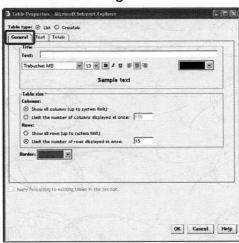

8

continued...

List – Table Properties

The Text tab in the Table Properties window for a list object allows you to select specific properties such as font style, size, and color for the following text in the table:

- headings
- subheadings
- cells

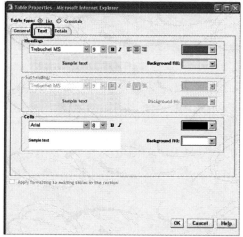

9

continued...

List – Table Properties

The Totals tab in the Table Properties window for a list object provides the mechanism to select the following:

- totals font style, color, size, and background fill color
- subtotals font style, color, size, and background fill color
- formatting

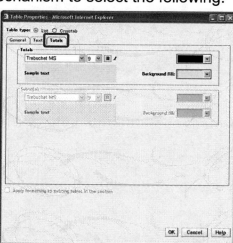

10

Report Objects – Crosstab

A crosstabulation (crosstab) table is a frequency table that shows combined frequency distributions or other descriptive statistics for two or more columns.

Both columns and rows are labeled in a crosstab table.

Customer Gender	Female	Male
	Customer Age	Customer Age
Customer Country		
Australia	42.503703704	44.346072187
Belgium	46.472727273	45.014218009
Benin	.	28
Bulgaria	.	31
Canada	39.80952381	42.725490196
Croatia	65	46
Denmark	43.137931034	42.463768116
Finland	43.903225806	42.714285714
France	42.321212121	43.840779854
Germany	43.746285714	44.604757548
Greece		43.333333333
Hungary	57.5	44
Ireland	36	58.2
Israel		35.75
Italy	42.418681319	42.998194946

Rows 1 - 15 of 24

11

The Table Data and Table Properties windows for the Crosstab object are similar to those for the List object. See section 5 of this chapter for more information.

Report Objects – Bar Chart

A bar chart consists of a grid and some vertical or horizontal columns (bars). Each column represents quantitative data.

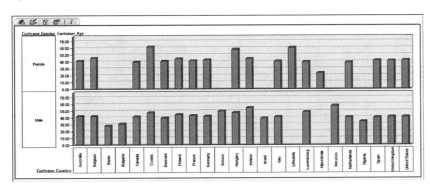

12

Bar Chart – Graph Data

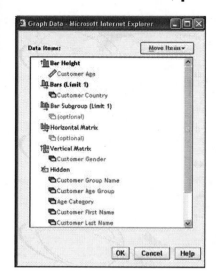

The Graph Data window for a Bar Chart object allows you to select the data item(s) used to represent the following:

- bar height
- number of bars
- bar subgroup
- horizontal or vertical matrix to separate the data in the graph
- hidden data items

13

Bar Chart – Graph Properties

The General tab in the Graph Properties window for a Bar Chart object allows you to select the following:

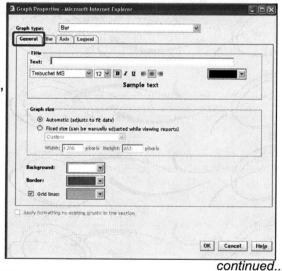

- title text, font style, size, color, and alignment
- graph size
- background, border, and grid color
- show grid lines
- formatting

14

continued...

Bar Chart – Graph Properties

The Bar tab in the Graph Properties window for a Bar Chart object allows you to select the following:

- orientation
- subgroup
- shape of bar
- show data values
- formatting

15

continued...

Bar Chart – Graph Properties

The Axis tab in the Graph Properties window for a Bar Chart object allows you to select the following:

- tick marks
- font style, size, and color for labels and data values
- label orientation
- formatting

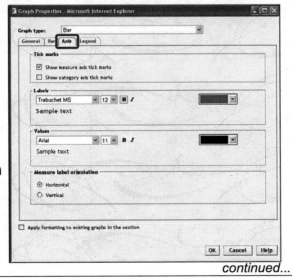

16

continued...

Bar Chart – Graph Properties

The Legend tab in the Graph Properties window for a Bar Chart object allows you to select the following:

- position of the legend
- font style, size, and color for labels
- formatting

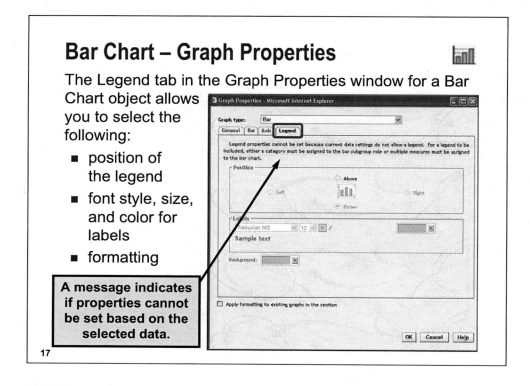

A message indicates if properties cannot be set based on the selected data.

17

Report Objects – Pie Chart

A pie chart is a circular chart that is divided into slices by radial lines. Each slice represents the relative contribution of each part to the whole.

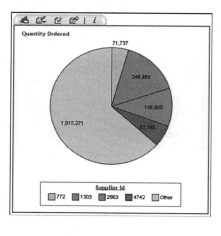

18

The Graph Data and Graph Properties windows for the Pie Chart and other chart/graph objects are similar to those for the Bar Chart object. See section 5 of this chapter for more information.

Report Objects – Line Graph

A line graph is a graph that shows the relationship of one variable to another, often showing movements or trends in the data over a period of time. Line graphs summarize source data and typically are used to chart response values against discrete categorical values.

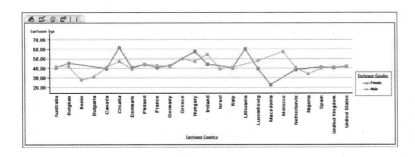

19

Report Objects – Bar-Line Chart

A bar-line chart is a bar chart with an overlaid line graph.

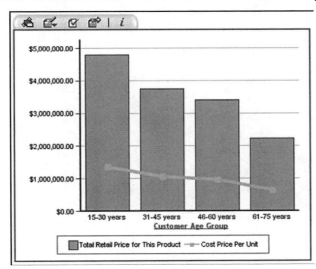

20

Report Objects – Progressive Bar Chart

A progressive bar chart is a type of bar chart that shows how the initial value of a measure data item increases or decreases during a series of operations or transactions.

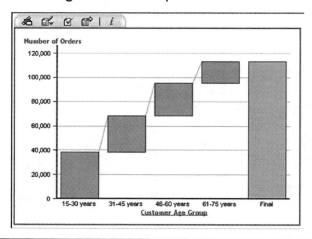

21

Report Objects – Scatter Plot

A scatter plot is a two- or three-dimensional plot that shows the crossing of two or three data items.

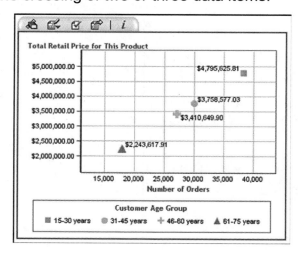

22

Report Objects – Geographical Map

The geographical map object enables you to display your OLAP data in an interactive geographical map.

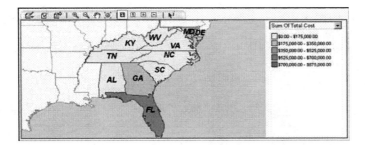

23

Report Objects – Text

Text objects can be used to display static text and can link to another report or a Web page. Text can also be used to display the items selected from dynamic prompt values.

The data in this report has been subset to only show orders for 2002.

Click here to view the Salary Analysis report.

This report is subset by Country - the currently selected values are: Germany France and Spain

24

Report Objects – Image

Image objects can be used to add static graphics to a report to help identify its use, such as information for the Shoe Division or worldwide sales information.

An Image object can also be set up so that clicking on it links to another report or a Web page.

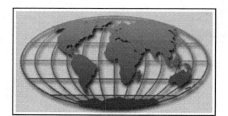

25

    For more information about importing images, see Appendix B.

Report Objects – Stored Process

A stored process is a SAS program stored on a server that executes and returns results to a report section. Because all of the instructions are part of the stored process, there is only one menu for the stored process object.

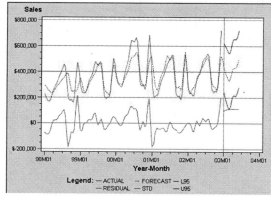

26

Add a New Section to an Existing Report

This demonstration shows how to use the Edit Report view to add a new section to an existing report.

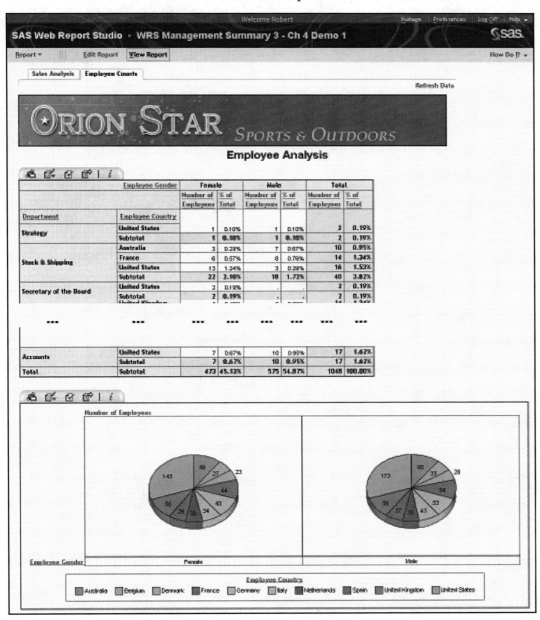

1. If necessary, open a browser window, select **Favorites** ➪ **SAS Web Report Studio**.

    a. Enter the user name and password provided by your instructor.

    b. Select ⎢ **Log On** ⎥ .

2. Open the **WRS Management Summary** report.

    a. Select **Report** ⇨ **Open ....**

    b. Open the **WRS Management Summary** report for editing by clicking on the actions button ([≡▾]).

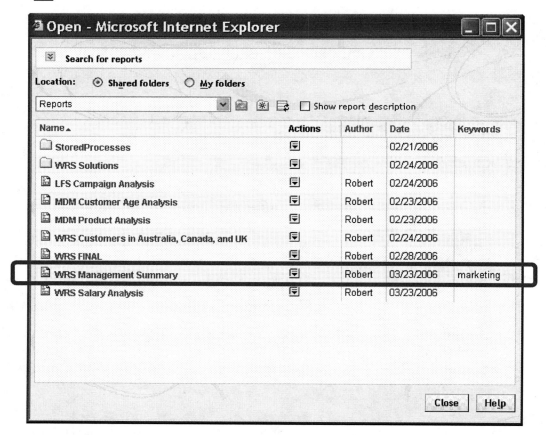

    c. Select **Edit....**

3. Because you will be adding a new section to this report, provide a meaningful name to the current section.

   a. Select **Section** ⇨ **Rename ...**.

   b. Enter **Sales Analysis** as the New section name.

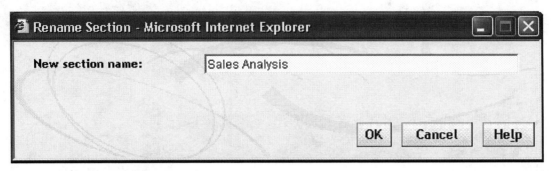

   c. Select OK to close the Rename Section window.

4. Add a new section to the report.

   a. Select **Section** ⇨ **New ...**.

   b. Enter **Employee Counts** as the New section name.

   c. Select **Get new data** in the Data area, because you will use a different data source for this section.

   d. In the Header area, select **Copy header from** and **Sales Analysis** to copy the header information from the existing section.

   e. Because there is no footer information in the current section, select **Blank** in the Footer area.

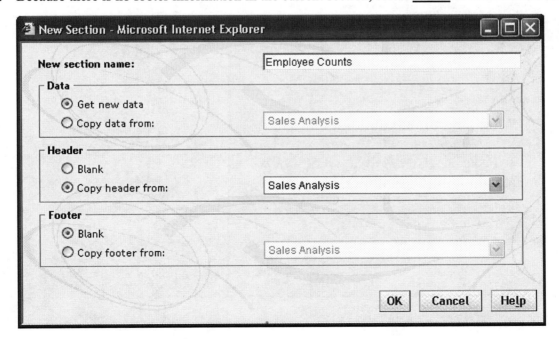

f. Select OK to close the New Section window.

The Edit Report view shows that there are now two sections and that the active section is Employee Counts.

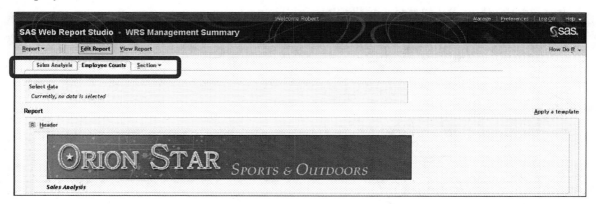

5. Select the data for the new section.

a. Select **Select data**.

b. Select **Change Source ...** ⇨ **WRS Organization**.

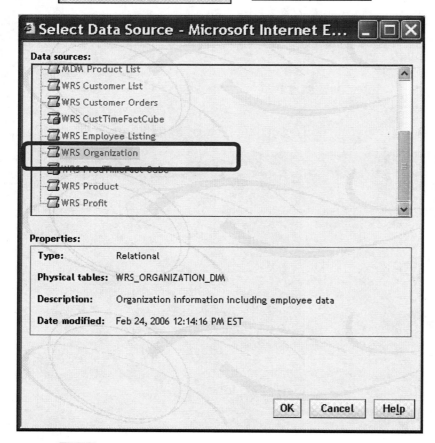

c. Select OK to close the Select Data Source window.

d. Select the following data items and move them from the `Available data items` list to the `Selected Items` list:

- **Annual Salary**
- **Company**
- **Department**
- **Group**
- **Section**
- **Employee Id**
- **Employee Name**
- **Employee Birth Date**
- **Employee Country**
- **Employee Gender**
- **Employee Hire Date**
- **Job Title**
- **Annual Salary** (a second time).

6. Scroll in the list of `Selected data items`, select **Annual Salary (2)**, and select the Rename Data Item (/) button.

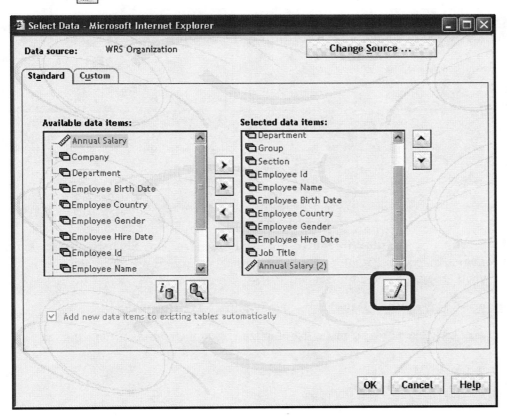

a.   Enter **Number of Employees** as the New name.

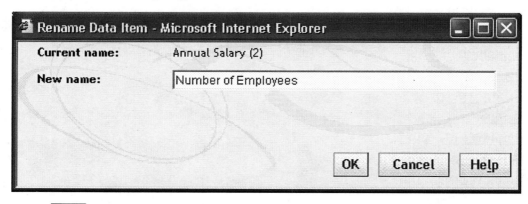

b.   Select **OK** to close the Rename Data Item window.

> ✎ This only changes the data item name; you will change the summarization level to count in a later step.

c.   Select **OK** to close the Select Data window and return to the Edit Report view.

d.   If necessary, select ⤓ to expand the Data area.

e.   In the Data area, scroll down to **Employee Gender**, and in the Filter column, select the predefined filter **Select a Gender**.

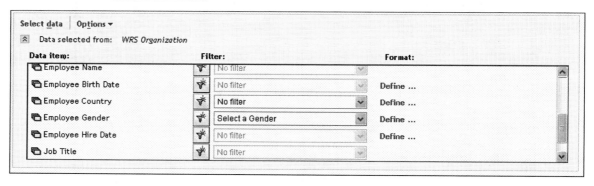

> ✎ The **Select a Gender** filter is part of the data source. This filter was created in the information map as a prompted filter – each time the report is refreshed, the user is prompted to select a value for Gender.

f.   Select **Options** ⇨ **Aggregate or Detail** to open the Aggregate or Detail window.

g.   Locate **Number of Employees** in the list of data items at the bottom of the window.

h. Select **Count** from the drop-down list for Aggregation.

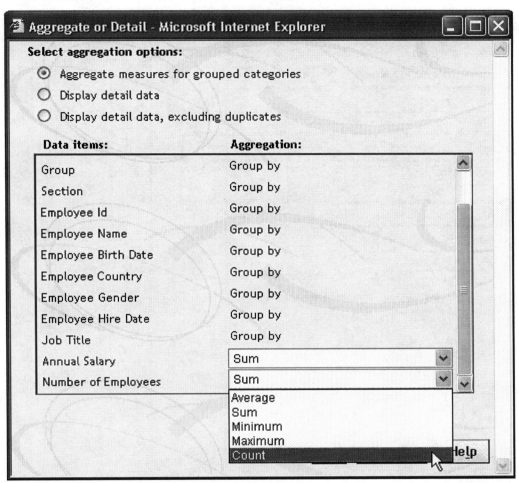

i. Select OK to close the Aggregate or Detail window.

✏ The Aggregate or Detail window is discussed in the next chapter.

j. In the Data area, scroll down to **Number of Employees**, and in the Format column, select **Define...**.

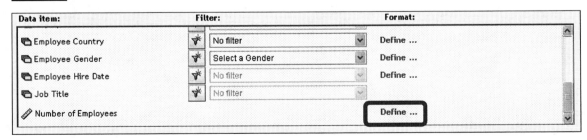

k. Change the `Type of format` to **Number**, the `Decimal places` to **0**, and select **Thousands separator (,)**.

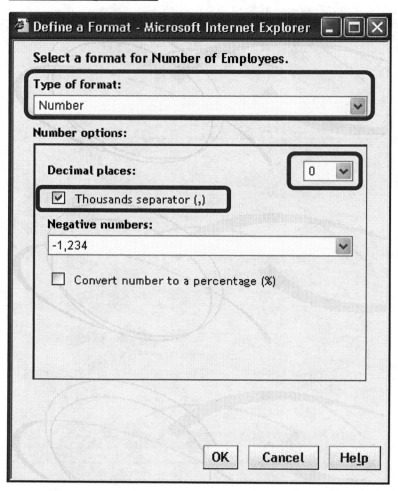

l. Select OK to close the Define a Format window.

m. Select ⊼ to collapse the Data area.

7. Update the header information.

    a. In the Report area, select Header

    b. Change the text to **Employee Analysis**.

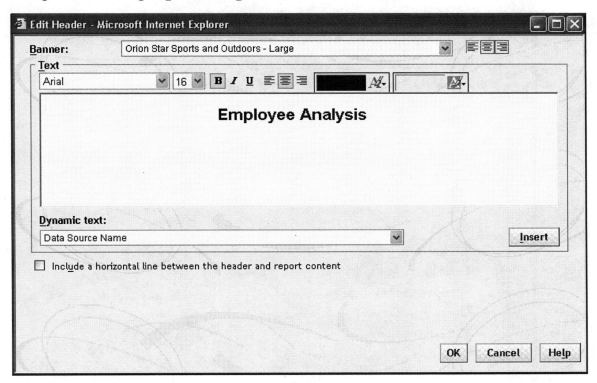

    c. Select **OK** to close the Edit Header window.

8. Add objects to the report.

    a. In the Report Object toolbar, select ▦ to add a Crosstab object.

    b. Select 🥧 and drag it under the Crosstab object to add a Pie Chart.

9. Specify the properties for the Crosstab.

a. Select 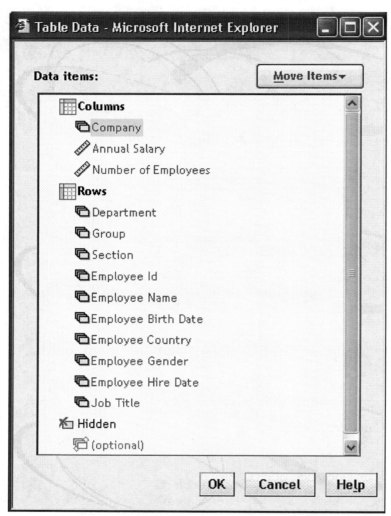 from the **Table1** toolbar to specify the Crosstab table data properties.

b. The first column is highlighted by default. Shift-click the last column (**Job Title**) in the Rows section to highlight all of the column names.

c.   Select **Move Items ▾** ⇨ **Move to Hidden**.

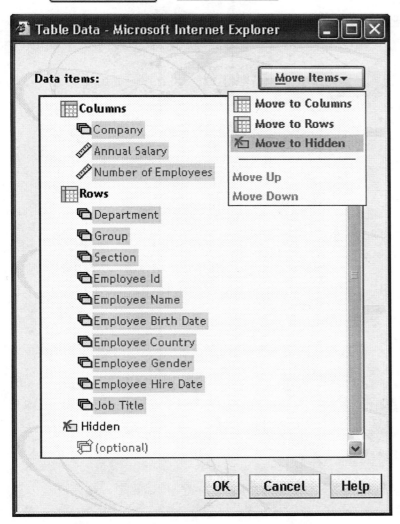

d.   In the **Hidden** section, hold down the CTRL key and click to select the following data items.

- **Employee Gender**
- **Number of Employees**

e. Select **Move Items▾** ⇨ **Move to Columns**.

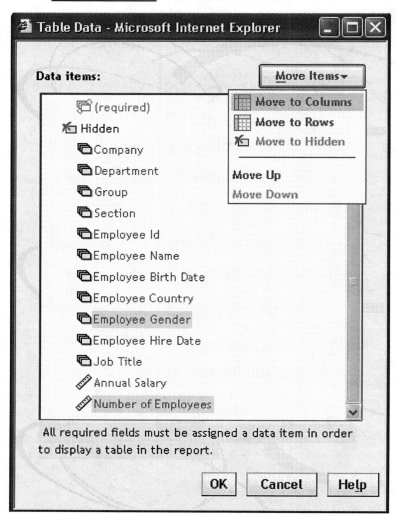

f. In the **Hidden** section, hold down the CTRL key and click to select the following data items.

- **Department**
- **Employee Country**.

g.   Select 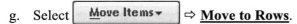 ⇨ **Move to Rows**.

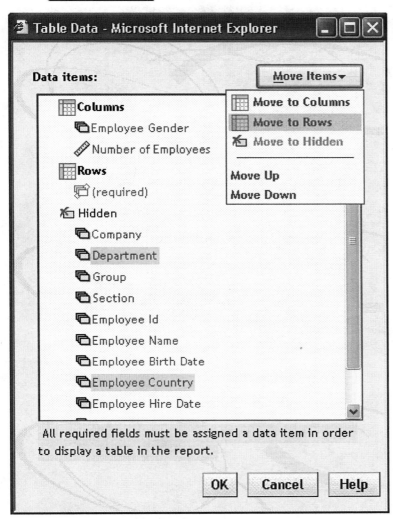

h.   Select | OK | to close the Table Data window.

i.   Add Totals and Subtotals to the report.

   1)   On the **Table1** toolbar, select ▨ and **Total...**.

   2)   Select **Totals** for the Rows.

3)   Select **<u>Subtotals</u>** and **<u>Totals</u>** for the Columns.

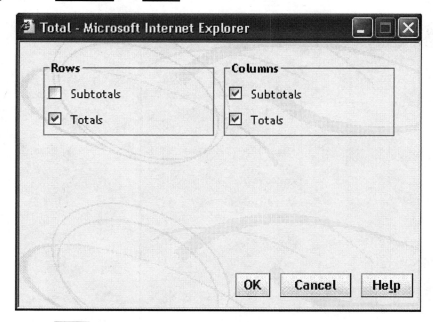

4)   Select OK to close the Total window.

j.   Add a new column that shows the percent of the grand total.

   1)   On the **Table1** toolbar, select 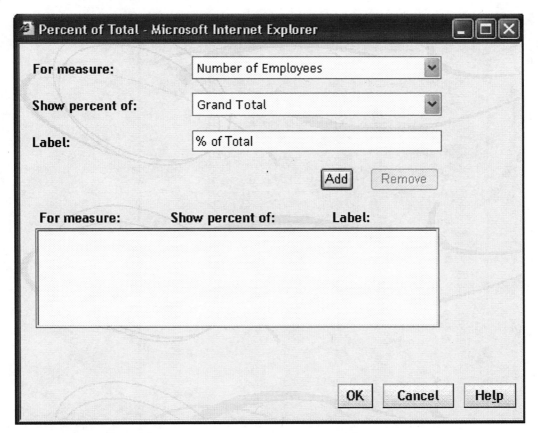 and **Percent of Total...**.

   2)   Select **Grand Total** as the value for Show percent of.

   3)   Enter **% of Total** as the Label.

   4)   Select [Add], then [OK] to close the Percent of Total window.

   ✎   This creates a new report column.

10. Specify the properties for the Pie Chart.

    a.   Select   from the **Graph1** toolbar to specify the Pie Chart graph data properties.

    b.   Select **Annual Salary** in the Segment Size section.

    c.   Select   Move Items▾   ⇨ **Move to Hidden**.

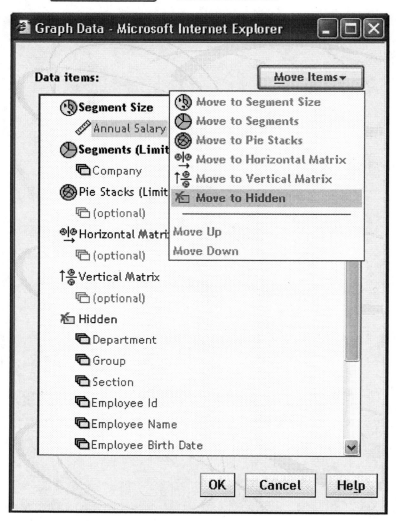

d. Select **Number of Employees** in the Hidden section and select 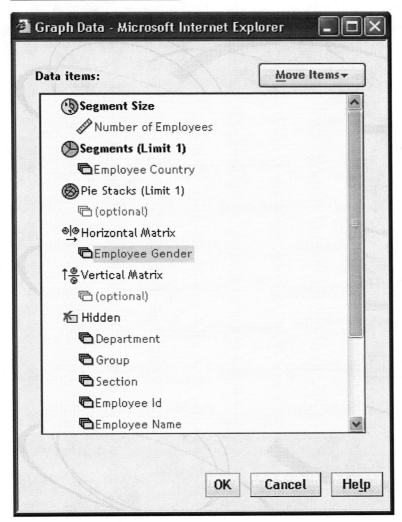 ⇨
    Move to Segment Size.

e. Select **Employee Country** in the Hidden section and select [Move Items ▾] ⇨
    Move to Segments.

> ✎ Because there can be only one data item in the Segments section, `Employee Country` replaces what was previously there.

f. Select **Employee Gender** in the Hidden section and select [Move Items ▾] ⇨
    Move to Horizontal Matrix.

g. Select [OK] to close the Graph Data window.

h. On the **Graph1** toolbar, select ☑ to open the Graph Properties window.

i. Select the **Pie** tab.

j. Select **Three-dimensional** in the Shape area and **Show data values**.

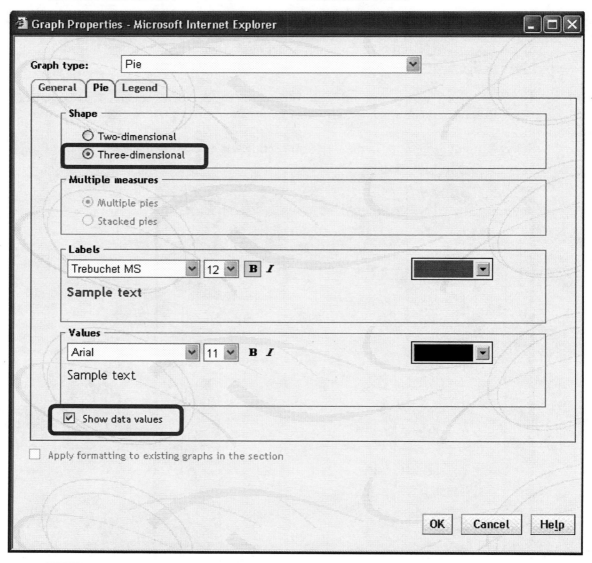

k. Select **OK** to close the Graph Properties window.

11. Enter new footer information.

a. In the Report area, select **Footer**.

b. Select **10 pt** as the font size.

c. Select ▤ to center the text.

d. Select **Report Name** from the Dynamic Text box at the bottom of the window and select **Insert**.

e. In the text area, type a space after **Report Name**, then type **report based on the** . Be sure to type in a space after **the**.

f. Select **Data Source Name** from the Dynamic Text box at the bottom of the window and select Insert .

g. In the text area, type a space and **data source** after the Data Source Name box.

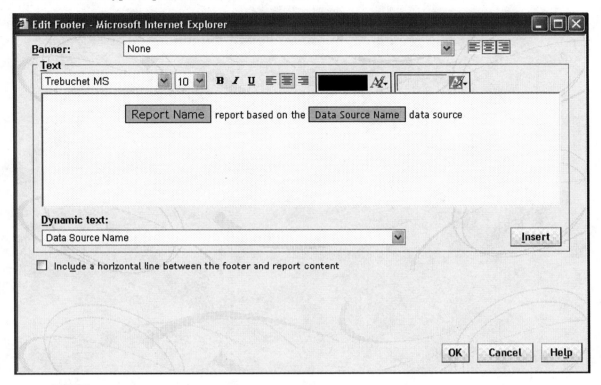

h. Select OK to close the Edit Footer window.

12. Select View Report to toggle to the View Report view.

a. A user prompt is displayed because you selected to use a predefined filter with a prompt. Select **Male** and ▶ to move it to the Selected values list.

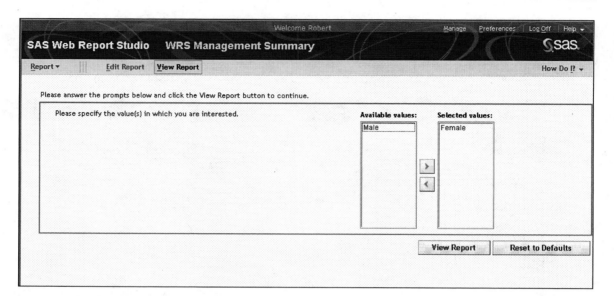

b. Select **View Report** .

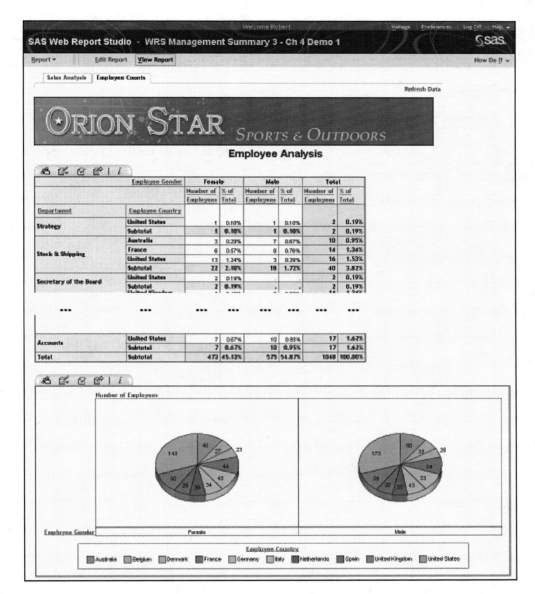

13. Sort the report by selecting the column heading **Department** ⇨ **Sort Descending**.

14. Save the report by selecting **Report** ⇨ **Save**.

Exercises

1. Adding a New Section to the WRS Management Summary Report

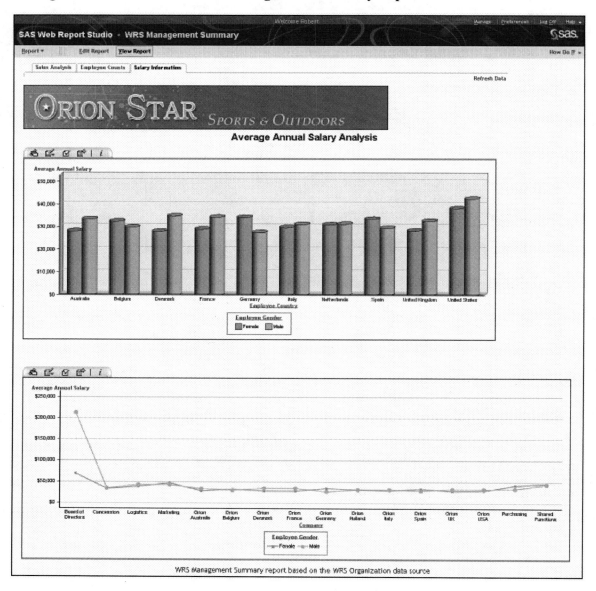

a. Log on to SAS Web Report Studio using the credentials provided by your instructor.

b. Open the WRS Management Summary report created in the demonstration.

> 🖉 If you did not follow along with the demonstration, create a new report from the last demonstration.

c. Use the Edit Report view to modify the report based on the following criteria:

- Add a new section named Salary Information.
- Copy the header and footer from the Employee Counts section (do not copy the data).
- Use the WRS Organization data source.
  - Select the following data items:
    - **Annual Salary**
    - **Company**
    - **Employee Country**
    - **Employee Gender**
  - Change the name of Annual Salary to Average Annual Salary.
  - Use the `Aggregate or detail` option in the Data area to change the default statistic of Average Annual Salary to Average.
- Change the text of the header to be Average Annual Salary Analysis.
- Add a Bar Chart object and a Line Graph object.
- Use the following properties for the bar chart.
  - Use **Average Annual Salary** to set the bar height.
  - Use **Employee Country** to create the bars.
  - Use **Employee Gender** to subgroup the bars.
  - Use clustered bars for subgrouping.
  - Use three-dimensional cylinders as the bar shape.
- Use the following properties for the line graph:
  - Use **Average Annual Salary** for the measure axis.
  - Use **Company** for the line.
  - Use **Employee Gender** to create multiple lines.

d. View the report in the View Report view.

e. Save the report replacing the previous version.

f. Log off of SAS Web Report Studio.

4.2   Using the Areas of the Edit Report View

Objectives

- Explore the options available in the Data area of the Edit Report view.
- Explore the options available in the Report area of the Edit Report view.

30

Edit Report View Areas

The Edit Report view has two areas for interacting with a report. The first is the Data area:

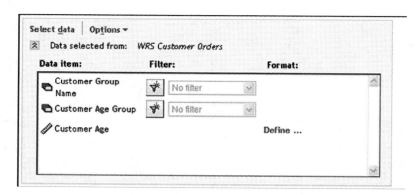

31   *continued...*

Edit Report View Areas

The second is the Report area:

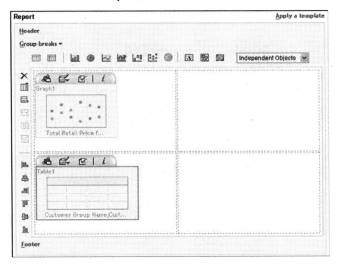

32

Edit Report View – Data Area

The Data area of the Edit Report view enables you to select a data source that will be used to provide data items to the objects in the report. When using a data source, you can do the following:

- add additional properties for each data item
  - select a pre-defined filter
  - create a new filter
  - apply a format
- specify other options for a data source

33

Selecting a Data Source and Data Items

When selecting data, you first select the data source and then select the data items.

Additional tasks are as follows:

- create custom data items for existing measure data items and simple mathematics
- rename data items
- move data items
- view properties for data items

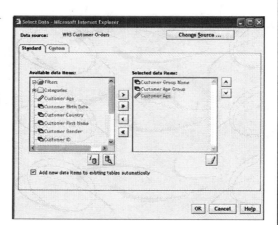

34

Creating Custom Data Items

The Custom tab of the Select Data window provides the ability to create new data items using existing measures to build basic expressions.

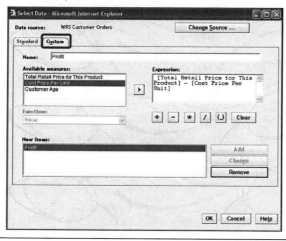

35

✎   Data item names can be up 56 characters in length and cannot contain the following characters: < > ( ) & # \

Filtering Data

Some data sources contain predefined filters for one or more data items.

To use a predefined filter, select it from the Filter drop-down list in the Data area.

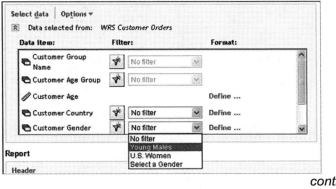

36   *continued...*

Only one filter can be selected for each data item.

Filtering Data

To create a new filter in SAS Web Report Studio, select the new filter button ⟨⟩ for the data item on which you want to create a filter.

The Create New Filter window allows you to perform the following tasks:

- provide a default name that you can change
- specify the filter operator
- provide options for entering values (based on options stored in the data source)

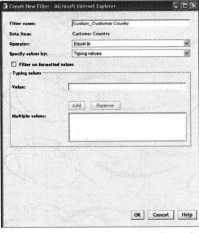

37   *continued...*

Filtering Data

Some data sources require you to enter a value manually while others allow you to select values from a list.

38

The ability to select values from a list is dependent on the settings in the data source.

Formatting Data

Some data items allow you to apply a format to the underlying data. A format provides instructions on how to display the data values in a report.

Some data sources store formats for specific data items.

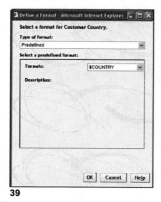 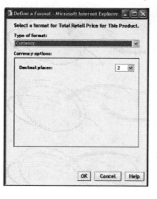 

39

The initial formats are inherited from the data source.

Data Area – Options

Selecting **Options** in the Data area allows you to perform the following tasks:

- create advanced filter combinations
- detail the filters being used
- choose how to group and summarize data
- select the summary statistic used for each measure
- preview data

40

Options – Filter Combination

Filter Combination allows you to choose how filters are applied. By default, data values must match all selected filters to be included in the report.

Selecting Advanced combinations allows you to specify how multiple filters are combined.

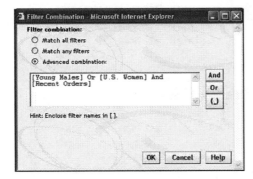

41

Options – Filter Summary

Filter Summary describes the filters that are applied to the current report section, which affect all of the tables, graphs, and maps in this section, as well as how the filters and rankings are applied.

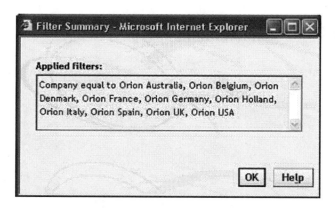

42

Options – Aggregate or Detail

Aggregate or Detail allows you to specify grouping and aggregation options for the results of a query that uses data items from a relational data source.

- **Aggregate measures for grouped categories** displays each distinct combination of values across all categories.

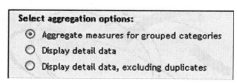

- **Display detail data** displays all rows.
- **Display detail data, excluding duplicates** displays all unique rows.

43   *continued...*

Options – Aggregate or Detail

Measures use the default aggregation specified in the data source. The Aggregate or Detail window enables you to change the summarization statistic for each data item.

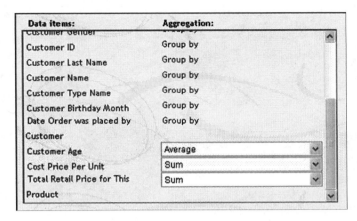

44

Edit Report View – Report Area

The Report area of the Edit Report view enables you to perform the following tasks:

- define header and footer information
- choose to break the report into groups based on one or more data items
- add and arrange report objects to the report grid by
  - selecting the object from the toolbar, or
  - dragging the item to a new location on the report grid, or
  - using a report template that contains layout information
- synchronize report objects

45

Report Area – Headers and Footers

Headers and footers provide the ability to have multiple types of information used at the top and bottom of each page of a report section. Items that can be used in headers and footers include the following:

- banner images
- static text
- dynamic text
- horizontal lines between the report content and the header and/or footer

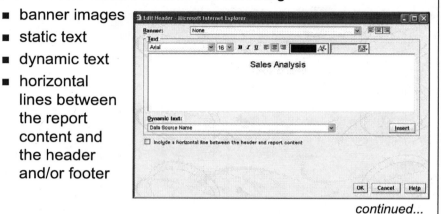

46

continued...

Report Area – Headers and Footers

The dynamic text that can be used in headers and footers includes all of the following:

- data source name
- data source description
- date the data was last refreshed
- report author
- report date
- report description
- report name

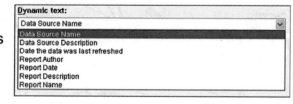

47

Report Area – Group Breaks

Reports can be organized into separate groups based on the values of one or more data items.

When specifying a group break you can choose the following:

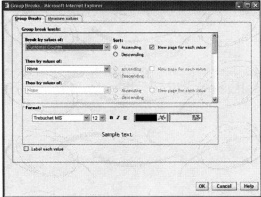

- sort sequence
- a new page for each value or keep the groups on the same page
- labels for each group value
- multiple text properties for group labels

48

continued...

Report Area – Group Breaks

A navigation window is created for reports with group breaks when they include the option to have a new page for each value.

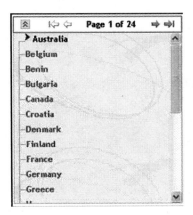

The navigation window provides an easy way to jump to each group of information.

Select ⤓ to collapse the navigation window and allow more room for the report.

49

Report Area – Adding Report Objects

Report objects can be added to the report grid by selecting them from the Report Objects toolbar.

After objects have been added to the report grid, they can be arranged by selecting and dragging to the desired location.

50

Report Area – Report Grid

Within the report grid, you can perform the following tasks:

- delete objects ✕
- add columns
- add rows
- merge cells
- split cells vertically
- split cells horizontally
- left-align object
- center object vertically
- right-align object
- align object at the top of the cell
- center object horizontally
- align object at the bottom of the cell

51

Report Area – Using Templates

SAS Web Report Studio has several predefined templates.

Templates contain layout information but do not contain data.

You can also create new templates. Templates can also be used when creating reports in the Edit Report view.

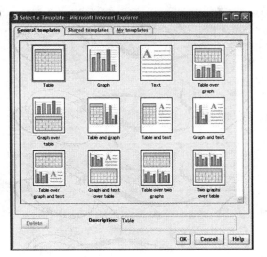

52

When saving a report, you can choose to save the layout information as a template that can be used for future reports.

Templates do not contain data or group breaks.

The following information is saved in a template:

- report tables and properties
- report graphs and properties
- images, properties, and linking information
- text objects, properties, and linking information
- headers and footers
- positioning information

Report Area – Synchronizing Objects

When building reports in the Edit Report view, you can choose to synchronize the objects in the report grid. Synchronized objects share category-based filters, sorting, drilling, and expanding.

To synchronize objects in the report, select **Synchronized Objects** in the Report Objects menu.

By default, report sections that are based on multidimensional data sources contain synchronized objects.

53

When you switch objects from independent to synchronized, the following actions are taken on any tables and graphs in the group:

- all filters and ranks are removed
- all sorting is removed
- tables and graphs are reset to the highest level drill state
- percent of total information is removed

Drilling and expanding are discussed in the next section.

Modify an Existing Section of a Multi-Section Report

This demonstration shows how to use the Edit Report view to modify an existing section of a multi-section report by synchronizing a table and a graph as well as changing some object properties.

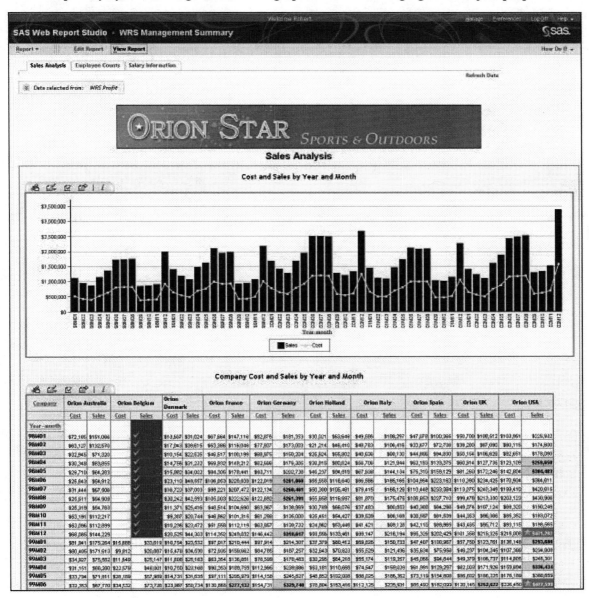

1. If necessary, open a browser window, select **Favorites** ⇨ **SAS Web Report Studio**, enter the user name and password provided by your instructor, and select   Log On   .

2. Open the **WRS Management Summary** report.

a. Select **Report** ⇨ **Open ....**

b. Open the **WRS Management Summary** report for editing by clicking on the actions button
    ().

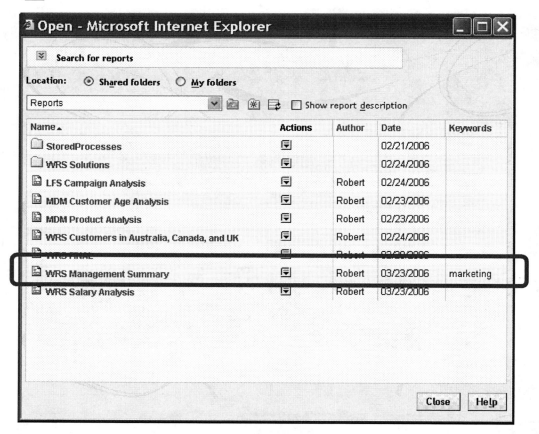

c. Select **Edit....**

3. Select the **Sales Analysis** tab to edit that section of the report.

4. The report currently has one Bar Chart and one Crosstab that are both independent objects. Make these dependent objects.

    a. On the Report Objects toolbar, select **Synchronized Objects**.

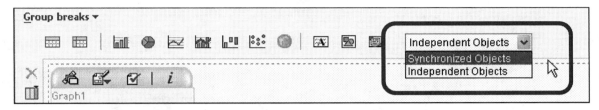

    b. Select [OK] in the message box.

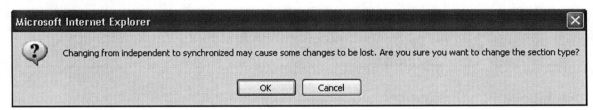

    The report grid in the Reports area shows a gray dashed line around both objects (around the blue border box) to indicate that they are synchronized.

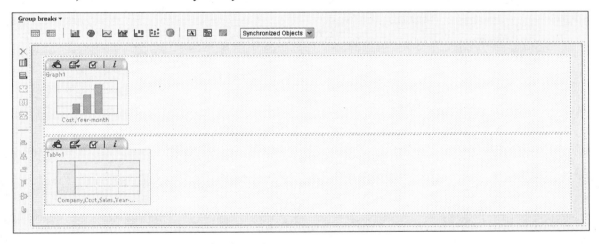

5. Change the Bar Chart to a Bar-Line Chart.

   a. On the Graph1 toolbar, select the Graph properties icon (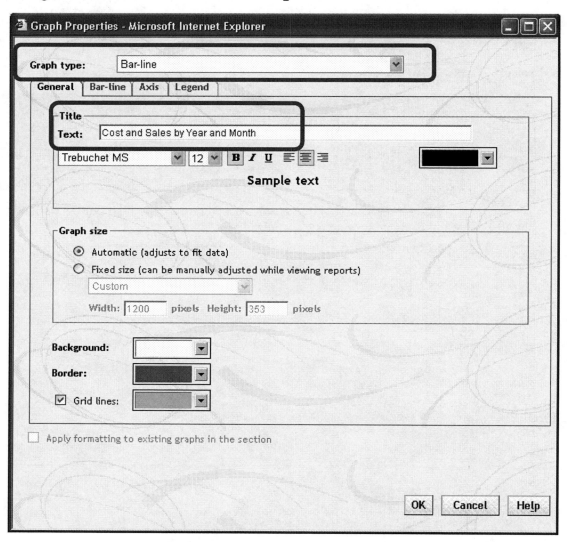) to open the Graph Properties window.

   b. In the drop-down box at the top of the window, change the `Graph type` to **Bar-Line**.

   c. Verify that the **General** tab is selected.

   d. Change the `Title` to **Cost and Sales by Year and Month**.

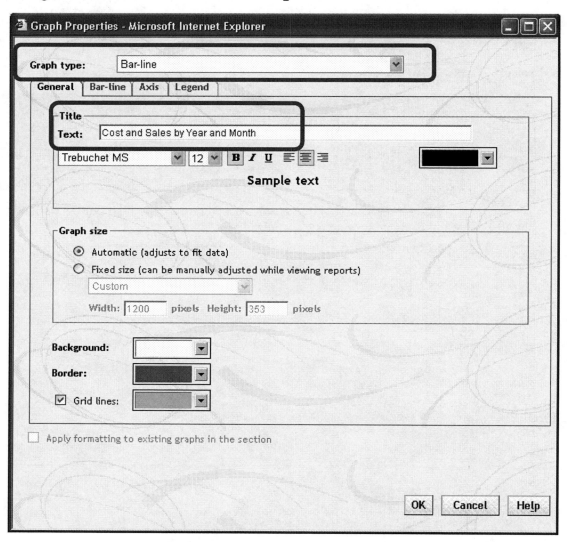

e. Select the **Bar-line** tab.

f. Change the `Bar shape` to **Three-dimensional bar**.

g. Change the `Bar color` to royal blue.

h. Change the `Line color` to bright yellow.

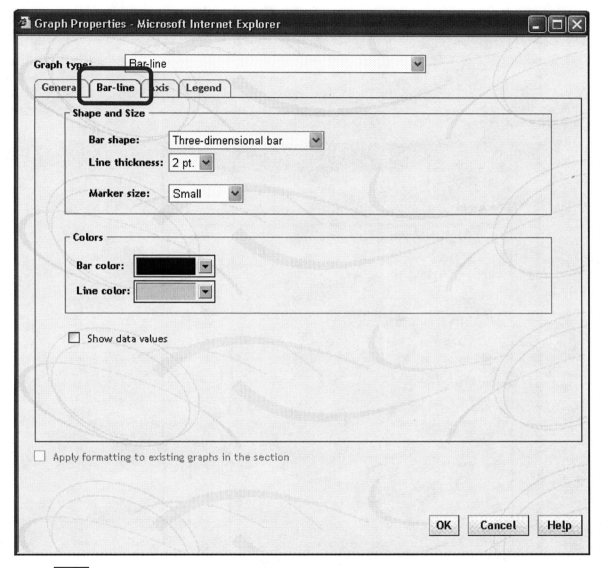

i. Select OK to close the Graph Properties window.

The graph object in the report grid has a warning icon to indicate that it does not have all of the required information.

j.   Select  to open the Graph Data window.

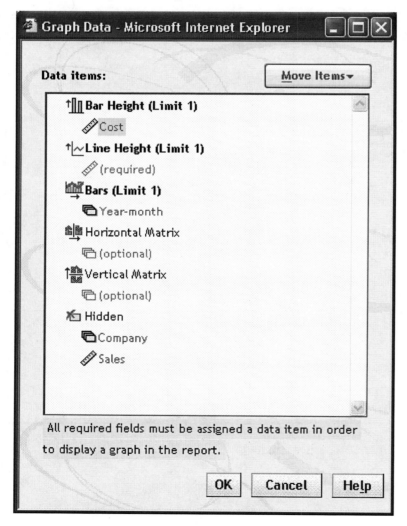

The note at the bottom of the window explains the reason for the warning icon. When you changed this from a Bar Chart to a Bar-Line Chart, there was no value automatically assigned to the Line Height.

k. Select **Cost** ⇨ | **Move Items ▾** | ⇨ **Move to Line Height**.

l. Select **Sales** ⇨ | **Move Items ▾** | ⇨ **Move to Bar Height**.

m. Select | **OK** | to close the Graph Data window.

n. Select | **View Report** | to toggle to View Report view and see the changes.

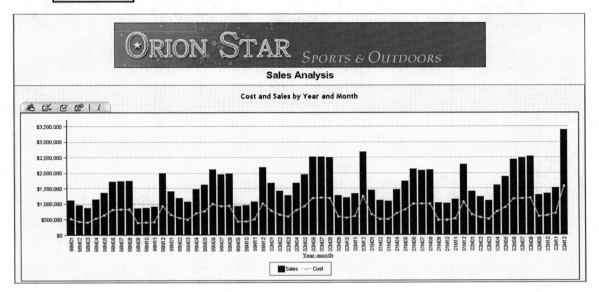

6. Apply Conditional Highlighting to the Crosstab to identify specific sales values.

    a. Select Edit Report to toggle to the Edit Report view in order to update the Crosstab.

    b. On the table toolbar, select ✎ and **Conditional Highlighting…**.

    c. To define a new rule, select New….

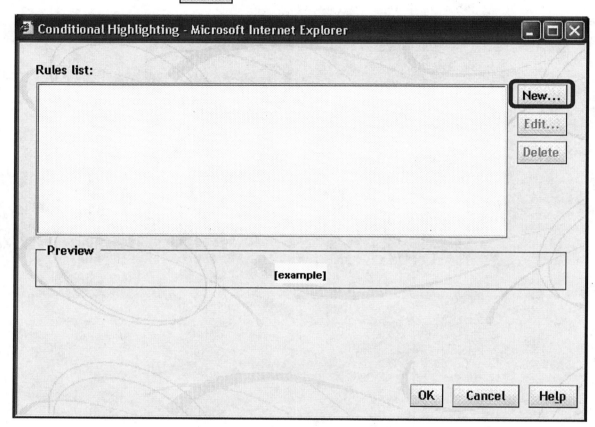

1) Select **Sales** as the Measure.

2) Select **Less than** as the Condition.

3) Enter **10000** as the Value.

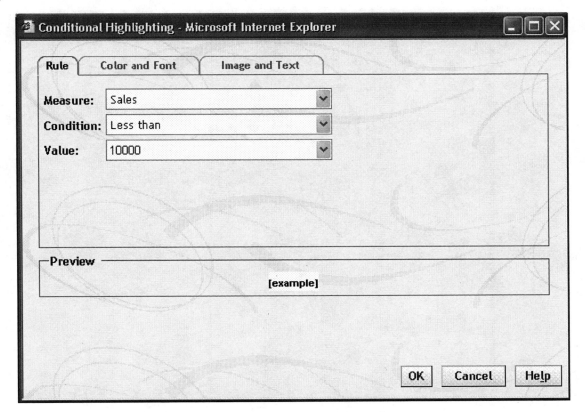

4) Select the **<u>Color and Font</u>** tab.

5) Select a Font color (first box) of white.

6) Select a Fill color (second box) of red.

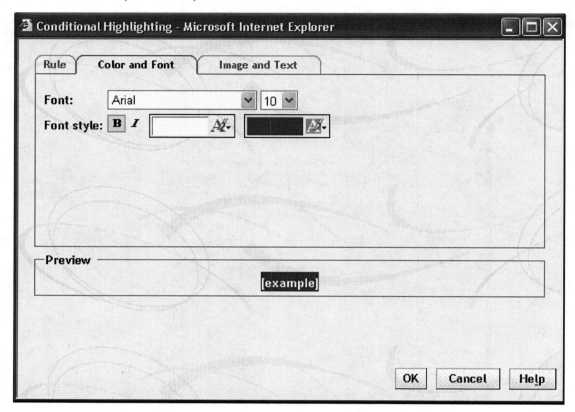

7) Select the **Image and Text** tab.

8) Select **Highlight by adding an image or text**.

9) Select **Image** as the value for Add.

10) Select **To left of cell value** as the Position.

11) Select the yellow checkmark (✓) as the Image.

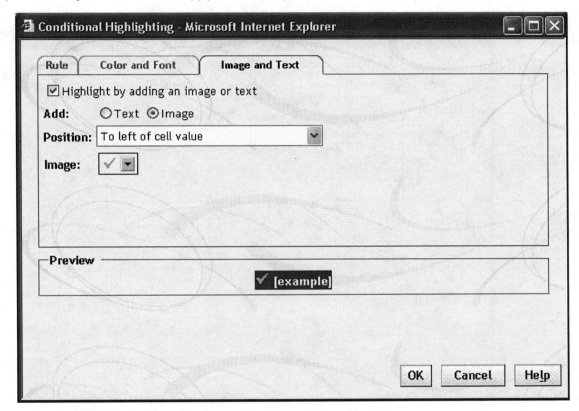

12) Select OK to close the Conditional Highlighting window.

d. To define a second new rule, select   New... .

   1) Select **Sales** as the Measure.

   2) Select **Is between** as the Condition.

   3) Enter **250000** as the Min Value.

   4) Enter **350000** as the Max Value.

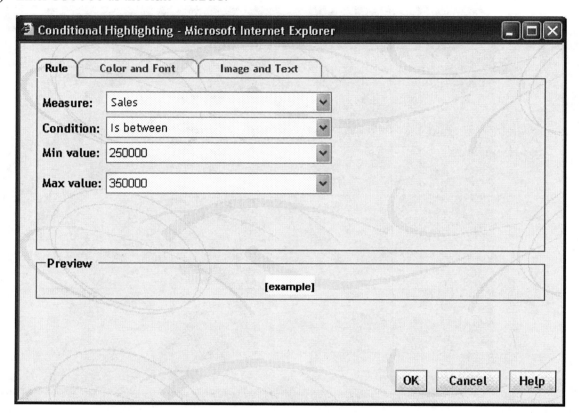

5) Select the **<u>Color and Font</u>** tab.

6) Select a Fill color (second box) of yellow.

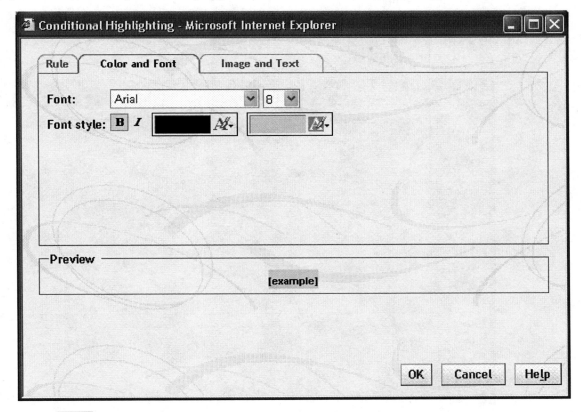

7) Select OK to close the Conditional Highlighting window.

e. To define a third new rule, select New... .

   1) Select **Sales** as the Measure.

   2) Select **Greater than** as the Condition.

   3) Enter **450000** as the Value.

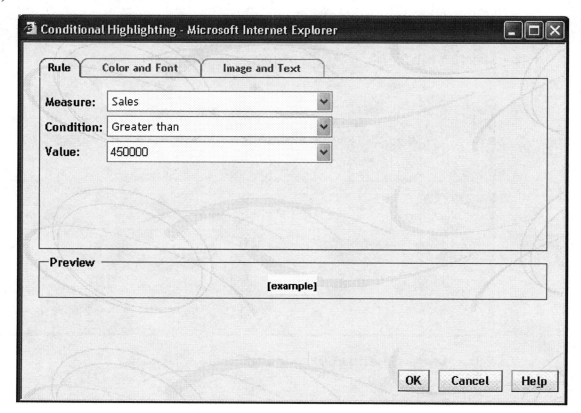

4) Select the **<u>Color and Font</u>** tab.

5) Select a Font color (first box) of white.

6) Select a Fill color (second box) of green.

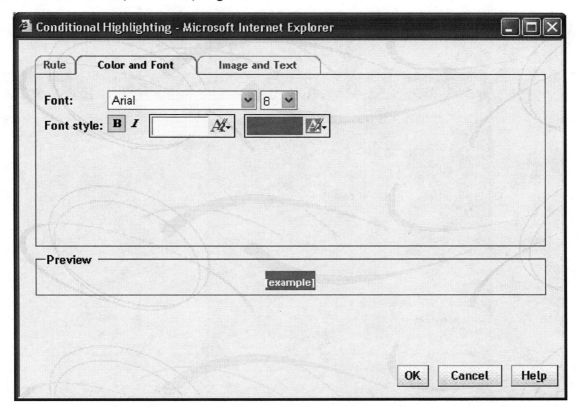

7) Select the **Image and Text** tab.

8) Select the **Highlight by adding and image or text**.

9) Select **Image** as the value to Add.

10) Select **To left of cell value** as the Position.

11) Select the yellow star (★) as the Image.

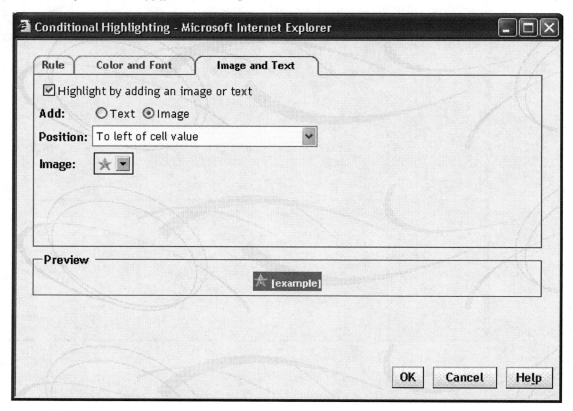

12) Select OK to close the Conditional Highlighting window.

f.   To apply the three conditional highlights, select OK .

g.   Select **View Report** to toggle to View Report view and see the changes.

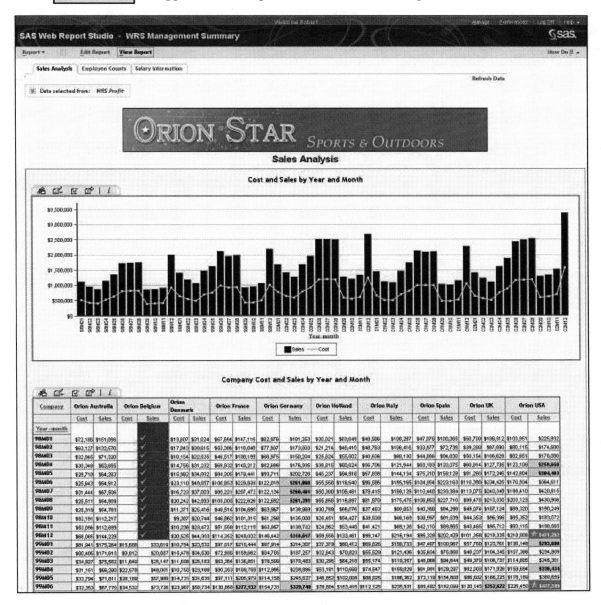

7.   Save the report by selecting **Report** ⇨ **Save**.

8. Save the report as a template by selecting **Report** ⇨ **Save As …** .

✎   Because saving a template will remove the data references in the report, make sure you save
      the report first before saving it as a template.

a. Type **WRS Management Summary Template** for `Name`.

b. Select **Template** for the `Type`.

c. Select **My templates** in the `Save to` area.

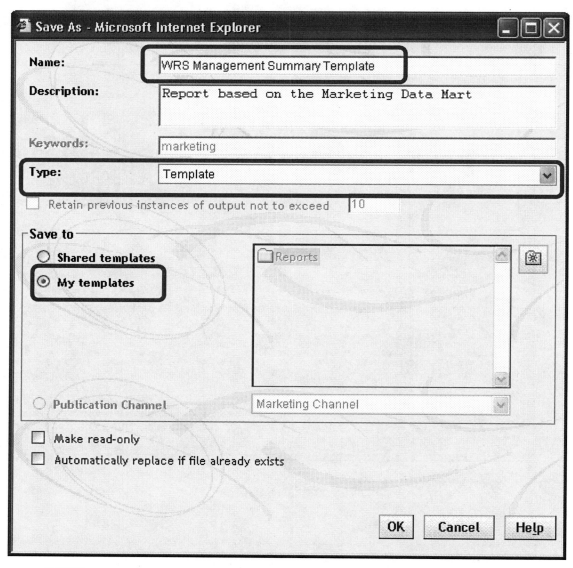

d. Select **OK** .

A dialog box notifies you that all data references will be removed in order to save as a template.

e. Select [OK] to save the template.

 **Exercises**

2. **Creating a New Synchronized Report** (using the criteria on the following page)

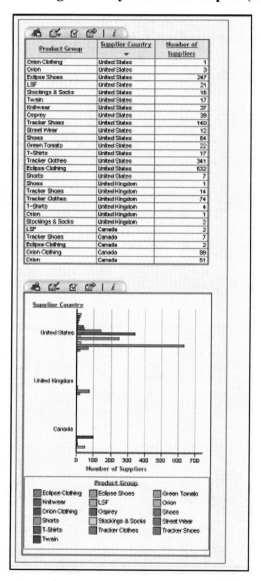

- Use the **WRS Product** data source.
- Select the following data items:
  - **Product Group**
  - **Supplier Id**
  - **Supplier Country**
- Change the name of **Supplier Id** to Number of Suppliers.
- Change the default statistic for **Number of Suppliers** to Count.
- Filter the **Supplier Country** to only include Canada, United Kingdom, and United States.
- Add a List object and a Bar Chart object.
- Synchronize the objects.
- Set the Properties for the List.
  - Columns from left to right are **Product Group**, **Supplier Country**, **Number of Suppliers**.
- Set the Properties for the Bar Chart.
  - Bar height – **Number of Suppliers**
  - Bars – **Supplier Country**
  - Bar Subgroup – **Product Group**
  - Horizontal bars
  - Three-dimensional bars
- Enter headers and footers of your choice.
- View the report.
- Resize the table columns.
- Sort the report in descending **Supplier Country**.
- Save the report in the Shared Folders as **WRS Supplier Count**.

4.3 Using a Multidimensional Data Source

Objectives

- Understand OLAP terminology.
- Use a multidimensional data source to build a report in SAS Web Report Studio.

57

What Is OLAP?

OLAP, or **O**n-**L**ine **A**nalytical **P**rocessing, is a technology that is used to create decision support software.

OLAP provides the following:
- multidimensional views of data
- calculation-intensive capabilities
  - ability to manipulate and derive data for analysis purposes across hierarchical levels
- fast access
  - gain insight into data through fast, consistent, interactive access to a wide variety of possible views of information
- time intelligence

58

What Is OLAP?

Central to the OLAP storage process are cubes.

A **cube** is a set of data that is organized and structured in a hierarchical, multidimensional arrangement, often with numerous dimensions and levels of data.

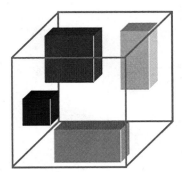

59

Terminology and Definitions

Cube	A logical set of data that is organized and structured in a hierarchical, multidimensional arrangement.

➢ A cube is a directory structure, not a single file.
➢ A cube includes measures, and can have numerous dimensions and levels of data.

60

Terminology and Definitions

Dimension	An organized set of categories, known as levels, that describes the data in data warehouse tables.

> **Examples:**
>
> **Time**
>
> **Product**

61

Terminology and Definitions

Level	One of the classification columns in a dimension hierarchy. Levels describe the dimension from the highest level (most summarized) to the lowest level (most detailed).

> **Examples:**
> **Time Dimension:**   Year
>   Month
>   Quarter
>   Day_of_Month
> **Product Dimension:**   Product_Line
>   Product_Group

62

Terminology and Definitions

Hierarchy	An arrangement of levels of a dimension that is based on parent-child relationships. Provides a navigational path that enables users to drill-down to increasing levels of detail.

> **Examples:**
>
> **YQM Hierarchy:**   **Year**
>   **Quarter**
>   **Month**
>
> **YMD Hierarchy:**   **Year**
>   **Month**
>   **Day_of_Month**

63

Terminology and Definitions

Measure	A special dimension that usually represents numeric values that are analyzed.

> **Examples:**
>
> **Cost**
>
> **Sales**

64

YQM Hierarchy

The YQM hierarchy was built to contain summary information by month, which can roll up into quarter, which can roll up into year. If the YQM hierarchy is used in an multidimensional data view, measures initially would be summarized at the year level.

	Sum of Sales	Average Sales
2002	xx	xx
2003	xx	xx
2004	xx	xx

65

continued...

YQM Hierarchy

Because the YQM hierarchy is used, year values can be broken down into quarter values.

		Sum of Sales	Average Sales
2002		xx	xx
2003	1	yy	yy
	2	yy	yy
	3	yy	yy
	4	yy	yy
2004		xx	xx

66

continued...

YQM Hierarchy

Similarly, quarter values can be broken down into months.

			Sum of Sales	Average Sales
2002			xx	xx
2003	1	Jan	zz	zz
		Feb	zz	zz
		Mar	zz	zz
	2		yy	yy
	3		yy	yy
	4		yy	yy
2004			xx	xx

67

OLAP Data in SAS Web Report Studio

Information maps can be defined on a SAS OLAP cube. These information maps are multidimensional data sources used to build reports in SAS Web Report Studio.

			Clothes		Shoes	
Product Category			Sum Of Sales	Average Sales	Sum Of Sales	Average Sales
Year	Quarter	Month Number				
1998			$1,149,066.98	$102.16	$1,248,130.80	$160.00
1999	1999Q1		$234,054.15	$77.19	$271,356.20	$118.14
	1999Q2		$376,442.28	$103.13	$425,132.68	$171.01
	1999Q3	7	$163,280.64	$133.84	$174,525.76	$217.88
		8	$151,936.81	$135.66	$167,647.92	$213.02
		9	$63,866.57	$85.16	$61,753.10	$126.54
	1999Q4		$347,557.71	$103.69	$289,246.56	$151.52
2000			$1,649,877.69	$103.83	$1,596,206.40	$156.88
2001			$1,403,518.10	$104.48	$1,305,060.74	$157.77
2002			$1,548,861.36	$105.58	$1,580,948.21	$160.75

68

continued...

OLAP Data in SAS Web Report Studio

Multidimensional data sources provide different ways to interact with reports that are not available with relational data sources.

If you want to ...	Then ...
Rotate the table	select the data item, and then **Rotate table**.
Drill down	select ⬇ next to the data item.
Expand	select ⊞ next to the data item.
View detail data represented by a value, row, or column	select the value, row heading, column heading, or name of the innermost member.

69

Create a Report from a Multidimensional Data Source

This demonstration shows how to create a report from a multidimensional data source.

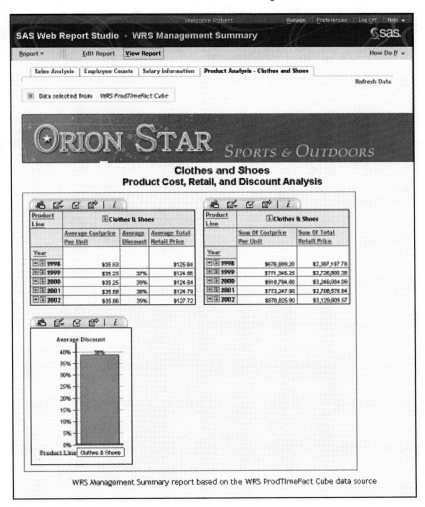

1. If necessary, open a browser window.

   a. Select **Favorites** ⇨ **SAS Web Report Studio**

   b. Enter the user name and password provided by your instructor.

   c. Select Log On .

2. Open the **WRS Management Summary** report.

    a. Select **Report** ⇨ **Open ...**.

    b. Select **WRS Management Summary** report by clicking on the report name to open the report in the View Report view.

3. Switch to the Edit Report view by selecting [**Edit Report**].

4. Select **Section** ⇨ **New** to create a new section.

    a. Enter **Product Analysis - Clothes and Shoes** as the New section name.

    b. Select **Get new data** in the Data area.

    c. Select **Copy header from:** ⇨ **Sales Analysis** in the Header area.

    d. Select **Copy footer from:** ⇨ **Employee Counts** in the Footer area.

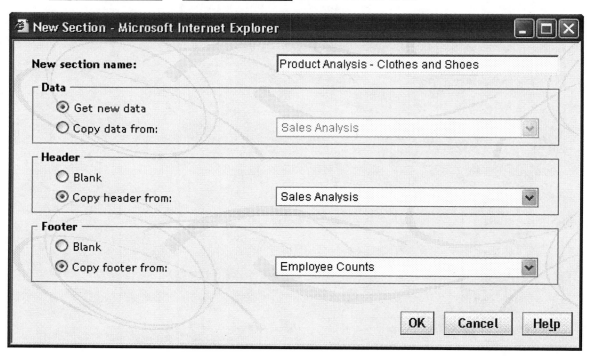

    e. Select [**OK**] to close the New Section window.

5. Select the data source.

    a. Select ⊻ to expand the Data area (if necessary).

    b. Select **Select Data** ⇨ | **Change Source ...** | ⇨ **WRS ProdTimeFact Cube** ⇨ | **OK** |.

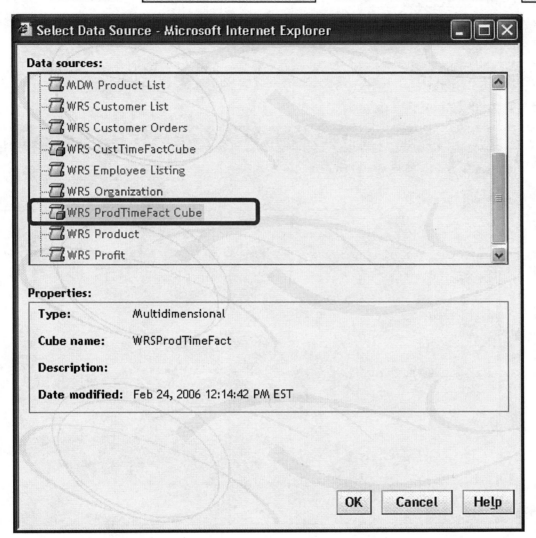

✎   The 🗂 icon indicates that this is a multidimensional data source. The data source type is
    also listed in the Properties type field. By default, report sections created from
    multidimensional data sources will have synchronized report objects.

6. Select the desired data items.

    a.   Select

- **Prod Hier (line, Cat, Grp)**
- **Time Hier (yr, Qtr, Mon)**
- **Average Costprice Per Unit**
- **Sum Of Costprice Per Unit**
- **Average Discount**
- **Sum Of Total Retail Price**
- **Average Total Retail price**.

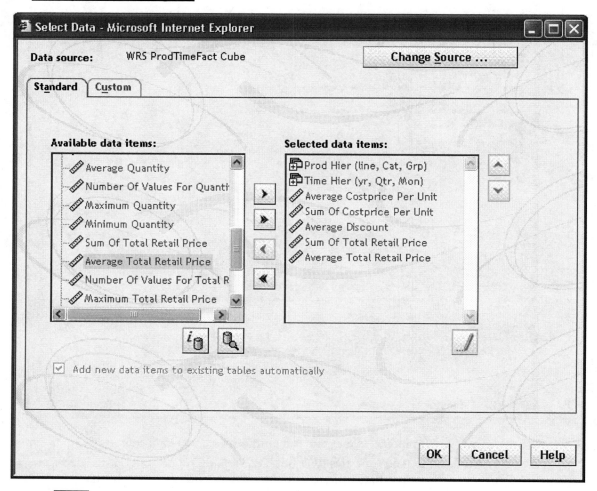

    b.   Select OK to close the Select Data window.

7. Update the header information.

    a. Select **Header**.

    b. Replace the existing text with **Clothes and Shoes**.

    c. Enter **Product Cost, Retail, and Discount Analysis** as the second line of the title.

    d. Select the second line of the title text and select a font size of **14 pt**.

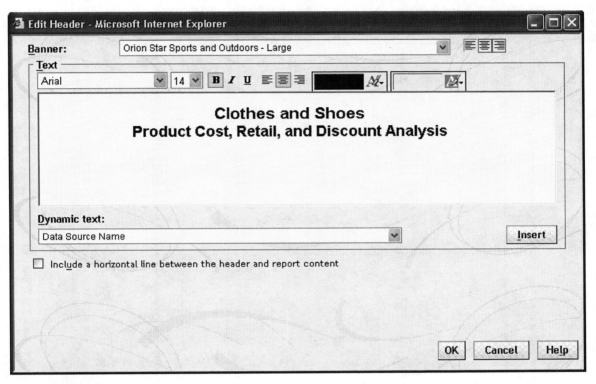

    e. Select **OK** to close the Edit Header window.

8. Add report objects to the Report grid.

    a. Select ▦ to add a Crosstab object in the first row of the report grid.

    b. Select ▦ to add a second Crosstab object in the first row of the report grid.

    c. Select ▥ to add a Bar Chart object and drag it below the first Crosstab object.

9. Set the properties for the first Crosstab object.

    a. Select 🖋 to open the Table Data window.

    b. Use the control-click method to select **Sum of Costprice Per Unit** and
        Sum Of Total Retail Price ⇨ | **Move Items▾** | ⇨ **Move to Hidden**.

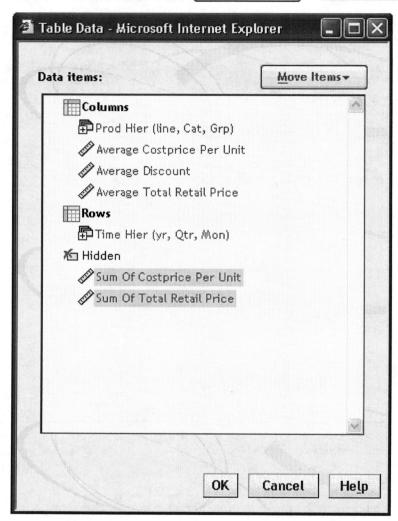

    c. Select | **OK** | to close the Table Data window.

10. Set the properties for the second Crosstab object.

    a.   Select 📇 to open the Table Data window.

    b.   Use the control-click method to select **Average Costprice Per Unit**, **Average Discount**, and **Average Total Retail Price** ⇨ Move Items▾ ⇨ **Move to Hidden**.

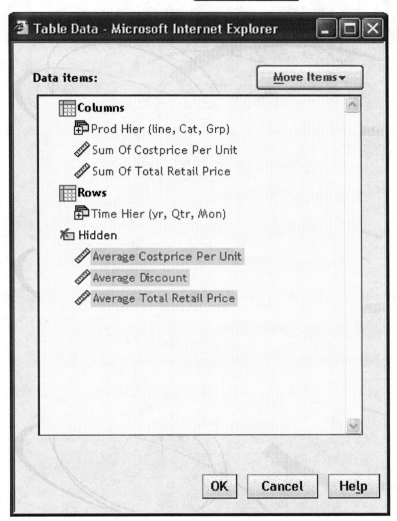

    c.   Select OK to close the Table Data window.

11. Set the properties for the Bar Chart object.

    a.   Select 🖳 to open the Graph Data window.

    b.   Select **Average CostPrice Per Unit** ⇨ [**Move Items ▾**] ⇨ **Move to Hidden**.

    c.   Select **Average Discount** ⇨ [**Move Items ▾**] ⇨ **Move to Bar Height**.

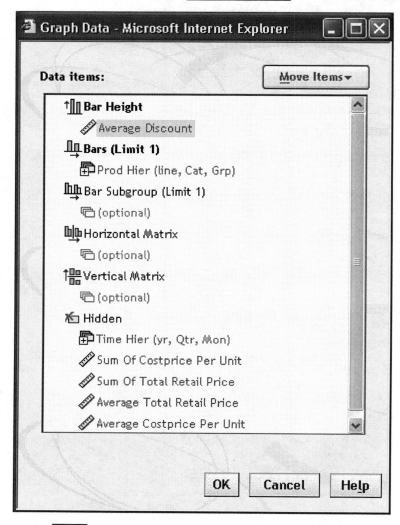

    d.   Select [**OK**] to close the Graph Data window.

e. Select 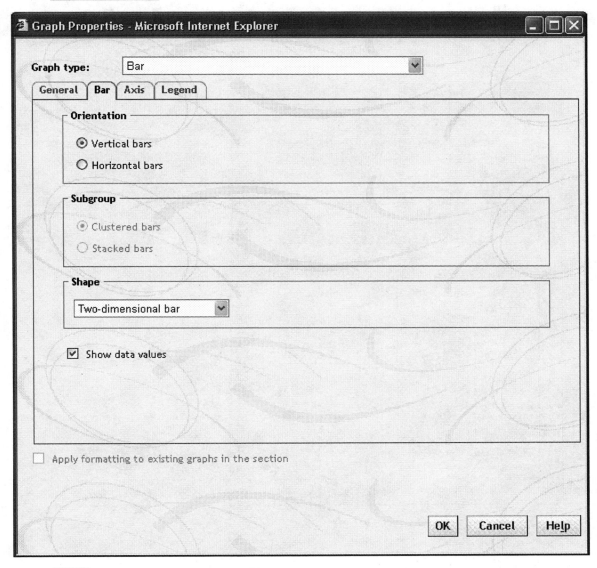 to open the Graph Properties window.

f. Select the **Bar** tab.

g. Select **Show data values**.

h. Select OK to close the Graph Properties window.

12. Select **View Report** to toggle to View Report view and see the new report.

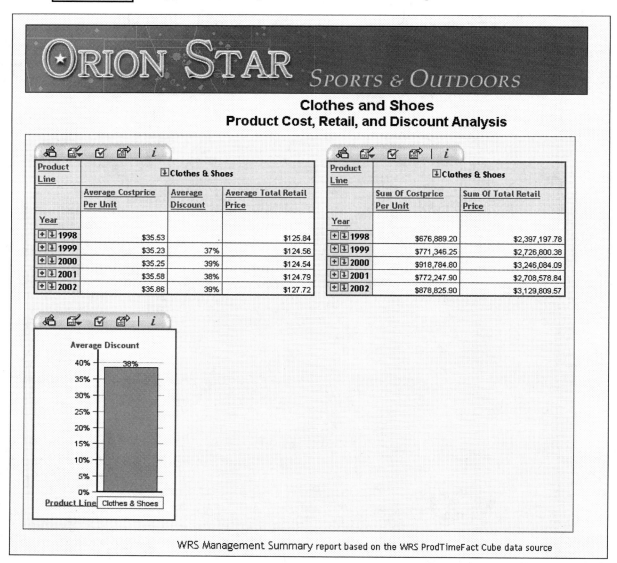

13. Select ⬇ for 1999 in the first table to drill down into the year 1999 data. Notice how the second table and graph reflect the changes since they are, by default, synchronized objects.

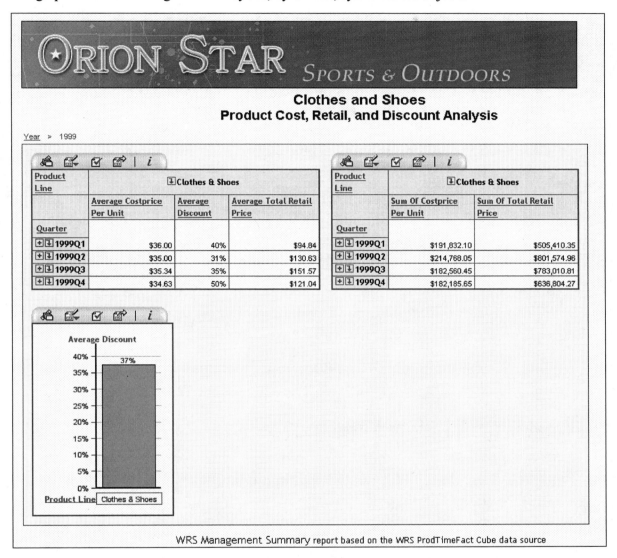

WRS Management Summary report based on the WRS ProdTimeFact Cube data source

14. To get back to the main report, select **Year** in the top left corner.

15. Save the report by selecting **Report** ⇨ **Save**.

4.4 Populating a Report Section with a Stored Process

Objectives

- Understand SAS Stored Processes.
- Use stored processes to build a section of a report in SAS Web Report Studio.
- Link a report.

72

What Is a SAS Stored Process?

A *stored process*

- is a SAS program that is hosted on a server and described by metadata
- can be executed by many of the SAS Intelligence Platform applications
- is similar in concept to programs run by SAS/IntrNet, but more versatile because of the underlying metadata and security support.

73

What Can a Stored Process Do?

Because a stored process is a SAS program, it can access any SAS data source or external file.

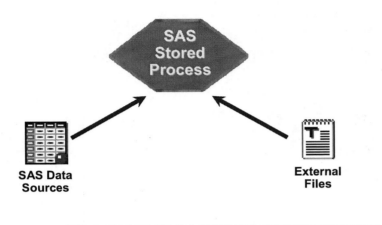

74   ...

What Can a Stored Process Do?

Because a stored process is a SAS program, it can create new data sets, files, and report output in a variety of formats.

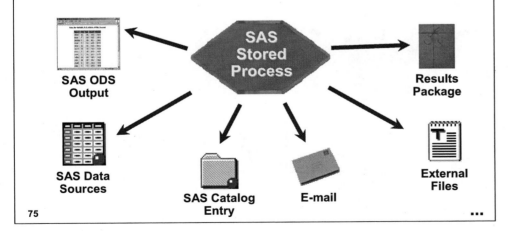

75   ...

Advantages of Stored Processes

SAS Stored Processes provides the following advantages over traditional SAS programs:

- code is not embedded into client applications
- programs ensure security and application integrity because the code is contained on a server
- code can be centrally maintained and managed from the server
- assurance that every client application that invokes a stored process always gets the latest version available
- ability for stored process programs to be invoked from multiple types of clients such as Web browsers and desktop applications

76

Methods for Invoking Stored Processes

Stored processes can be invoked from several of the SAS Intelligence Platform applications.

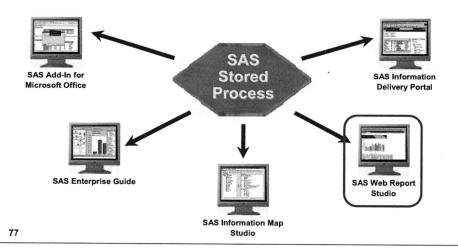

77

Stored Processes Metadata Structure

Metadata is used in stored processes to describe the following:

- input parameters
- input data sources
- output options
- execution environment
- descriptive data
- security options

78

Stored Processes and SAS Web Report Studio

To include a stored process in your report, select a stored process object into the report grid.

Stored processes must be registered in a specific location in the metadata to be available for use in SAS Web Report Studio.

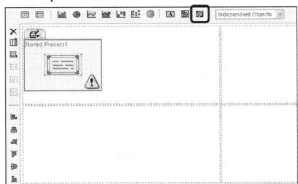

79

Metadata for stored processes must be stored in a specific location in the Metadata server. For more information, see Appendix B.

Stored Processes and SAS Web Report Studio

Stored processes provide the ability to include information in your report that you cannot get from the standard functionality of SAS Web Report Studio.

This report is built from a stored process that runs a SAS procedure to create a forecast report.

Stored processes allow this information to be included in a SAS Web Report Studio report.

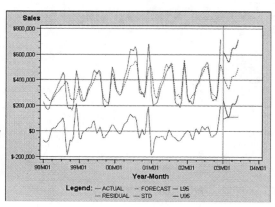

80

Use SAS Stored Processes to Create a Report Section

This demonstration shows how to create a section of a report with two stored processes and a report link.

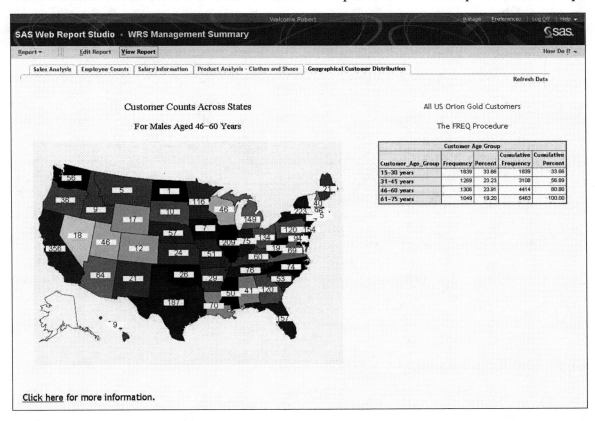

1. If necessary, open a browser window.

   a. Select **Favorites** ⇨ **SAS Web Report Studio**.

   b. Enter the user name and password provided by your instructor.

   c. Select **Log On** .

2. Open the **WRS Management Summary** report.

   a. Select **Report** ⇨ **Open ...**.

   b. Select **WRS Management Summary** report by clicking on the report name to open the report in the View Report view.

3. Switch to the Edit Report view by selecting **Edit Report** .

4. Select **Section** ⇨ **New** to create a new section.

    a. Enter **Geographical Customer Distribution** as the New section name.

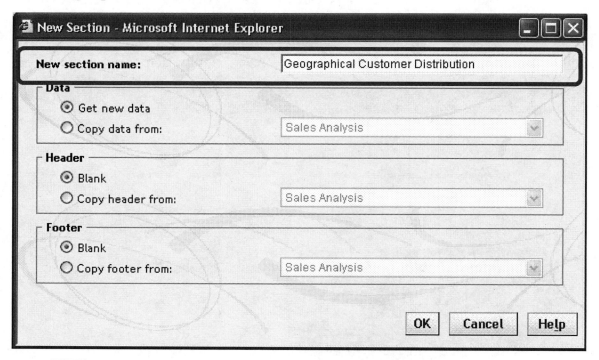

    b. Select | **OK** | to close the New Section window.

5. Insert stored processes.

    a. On the Report Object toolbar, select 🗐 to insert a stored process object.

    b. Click and drag 🗐 to insert a second stored process object to the right of the first stored process.

    c. The Stored process object in the report grid area has a warning icon to indicate that it does not have all of the required information.

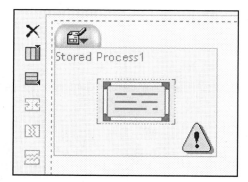

    d. Select 📝 ⇨ **Edit Stored process ...** for the first stored process object.

e. Select **Orion Customer Counts** and select OK .

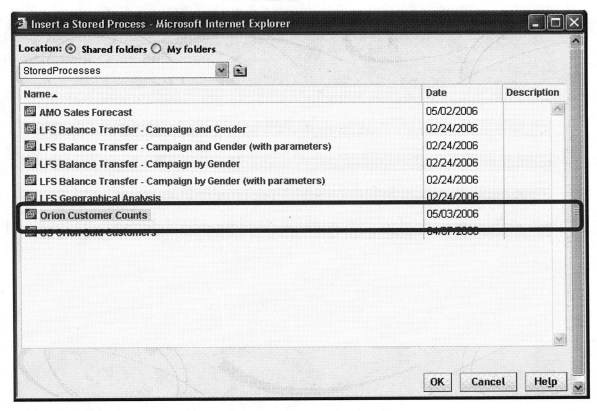

f. Select ![icon] ⇨ **Edit Stored process ...** for the second stored process object.

g.   Select **US Orion Gold Customers** and select OK .

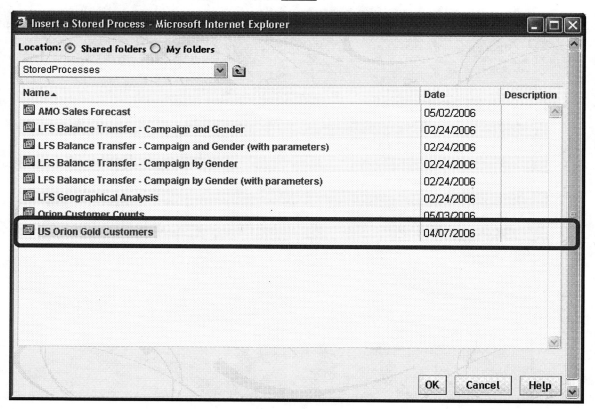

h.   Highlight the US Orion Gold Customers stored process object and select ⊞ to center align.

6.   Include a link to another report.

a.   In the Report grid, select ▣ to add a text box under the first stored process.

b.   Select ▤ ⇨ **Edit text ...** to open the Edit text window.

c.   Type `Click here for more information`.

d. Highlight the text **Click here** and select the Create a link (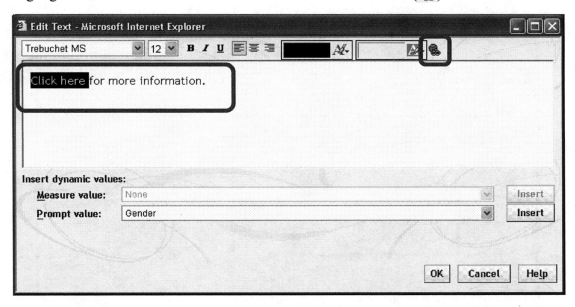) icon.

e. Select **Make text a link**, select **An existing report** for the Link destination, and select **WRS Customer Information**.

f. Type **More US Customer Data** for the `Tool-tip text.`

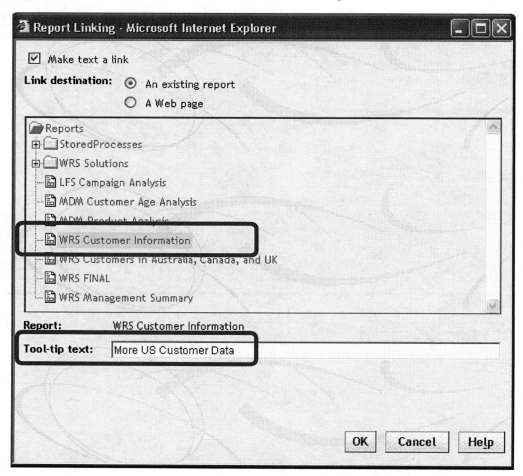

g. Select **OK** to close the Report Linking window.

h.   Highlight the text and change the font to **14pt**.

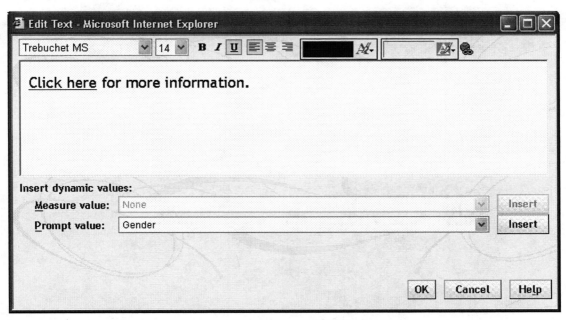

i.   Select **OK** to close the Edit Text window.

7.   Select **View Report** to view the report.

a.   The Orion Customer Counts stored process includes parameters. Select **M** as the value for
     Gender and **46-60 years** as the value for Age Group.

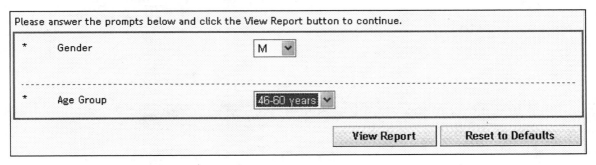

b. Select   **View Report**   .

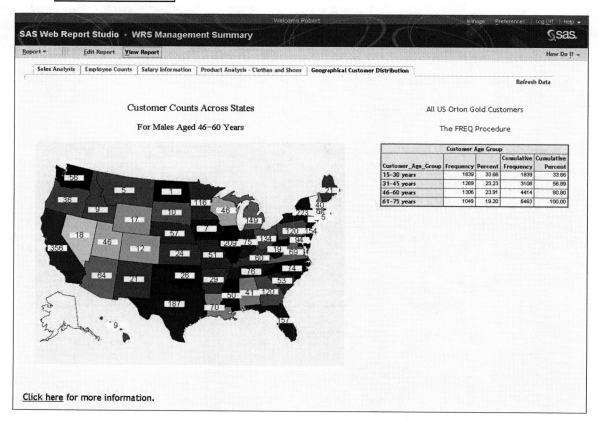

✎   To run the report again with different parameters, select **Refresh Data** in the top right corner.

c. Select **Click here** to see the linked report.

You may see this dialog box, prompting you to save your report before viewing the linked report.

d. If prompted, select [OK].

e. Select **Report** ⇨ **Save**.

f. Select **Click here** to see the linked report.

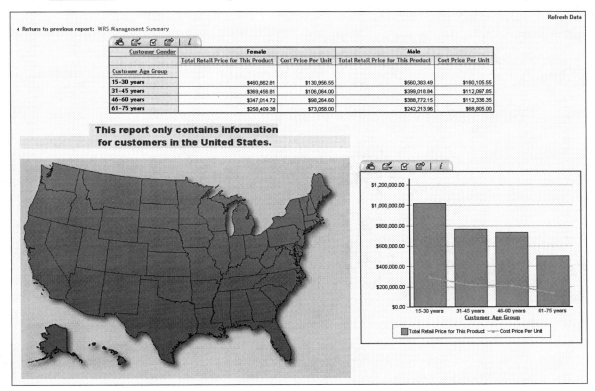

g. Select **Return to previous report: WRS Management Summary** in the top-left corner to return to the main report.

8. Save the report by selecting **Report** ⇨ **Save**.

4.5 Reference: Report Objects (Self-Study)

Report Objects – List

A list table is a two-dimensional representation of data in which the data values are arranged in unlabeled rows and labeled columns.

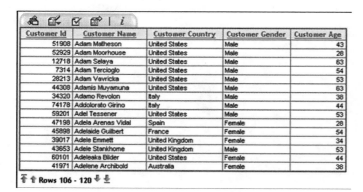

83

List – Table Data

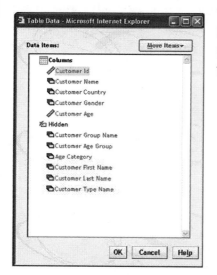

The Table Data window for a List object provides the mechanism to select the following:

- data items that populate the columns of the list table

- hidden data items

84

List – Table Properties

The General tab in the Table Properties window for a list object allows you to select the following:

- title text, font style, size, color, and alignment
- number of columns and rows to display
- border color
- formatting

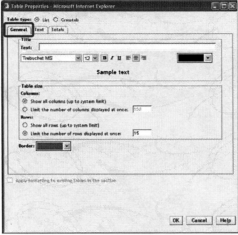

85

continued...

List – Table Properties

The Text tab in the Table Properties window for a list object allows you to select specific properties such as font style, size, and color for the following text in the table:

- headings
- subheadings
- cells

86

continued...

List – Table Properties

The Totals tab in the Table Properties window for a list object provides the mechanism to select the following:

- totals font style, color, size, and background fill color
- subtotals font style, color, size, and background fill color
- formatting

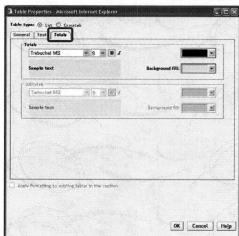

87

Report Objects – Crosstab

A crosstabulation (crosstab) table is a frequency table that shows combined frequency distributions or other descriptive statistics for two or more columns.

Both columns and rows are labeled in a crosstab table.

Customer Gender	Female	Male
	Customer Age	Customer Age
Customer Country		
Australia	42.503703704	44.346072187
Belgium	46.472727273	45.014218009
Benin		28
Bulgaria		31
Canada	39.80952381	42.725490196
Croatia	65	46
Denmark	43.137931034	42.463768116
Finland	43.903225806	42.714285714
France	42.321212121	43.840779654
Germany	43.746285714	44.804757548
Greece		43.333333333
Hungary	57.5	44
Ireland	36	58.2
Israel		35.75
Italy	42.418681319	42.998194946

Rows 1 - 15 of 24

88

Crosstab – Table Data

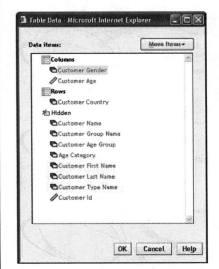

The Table Data window for a Crosstab object provides the mechanism to select the following:

- data items that populate the columns
- data items that populate the rows
- hidden data items

89

Crosstab – Table Properties

The General tab in the Table Properties window for a crosstab object provides the mechanism to select the following:

- title text, font style, size, color, and alignment
- number of columns and rows to display
- border color
- formatting

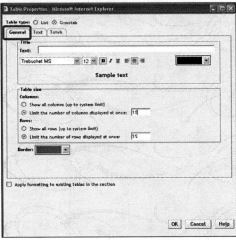

90

continued...

Crosstab – Table Properties

The Text tab in the Table Properties window for a crosslist object provides the mechanism to select specific

properties such as font style, size, and color for the following text in the table:

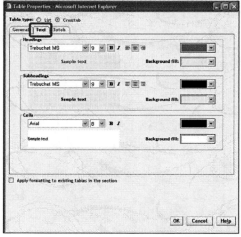

- headings
- subheadings
- cells

91

continued...

Crosstab – Table Properties

The Totals tab in the Table Properties window for a crosstab object provides the mechanism to select the following:

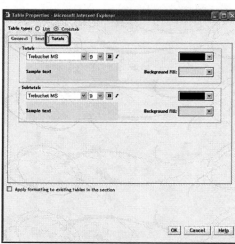

- totals font style, color, size, and background fill color
- subtotals font style, color, size, and background fill color
- formatting

92

Report Objects – Bar Chart

A bar chart consists of a grid and some vertical or horizontal columns (bars). Each column represents quantitative data.

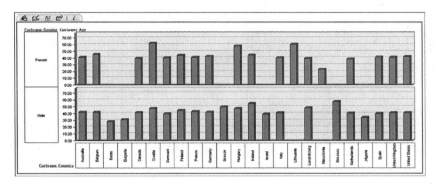

93

Bar Chart – Graph Data

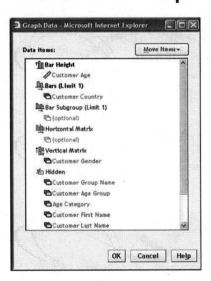

The Graph Data window for a Bar Chart object enables you to select the data item(s) used to represent the following:

- bar height
- number of bars
- bar subgroup
- horizontal or vertical matrix to separate the data in the graph
- hidden data items

94

Bar Chart – Graph Properties

The General tab in the Graph Properties window for a Bar Chart object enables you to select the following:

- title text, font style, size, color, and alignment
- graph size
- background, border, and grid color
- show grid lines
- formatting

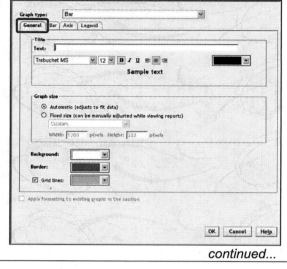

95

continued...

Bar Chart – Graph Properties

The Bar tab in the Graph Properties window for a Bar Chart object enables you to select the following:

- orientation
- subgroup
- shape of bar
- show data values
- formatting

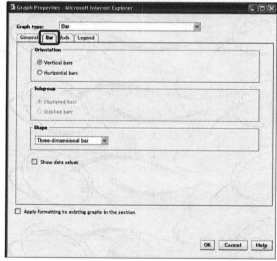

96

continued...

Bar Chart – Graph Properties

The Axis tab in the Graph Properties window for a Bar Chart object enables you to select the following:

- tick marks
- font style, size, and color for labels and data values
- label orientation
- formatting

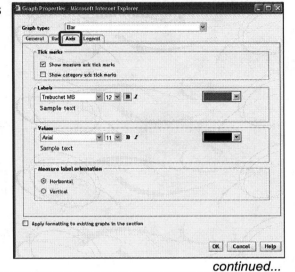

97

continued...

Bar Chart – Graph Properties

The Legend tab in the Graph Properties window for a Bar Chart object enables you to select the following:

- position of the legend
- font style, size, and color for labels
- formatting

A message indicates if properties cannot be set based on the selected data.

98

Report Objects – Pie Chart

A pie chart is a circular chart that is divided into slices by radial lines. Each slice represents the relative contribution of each part to the whole.

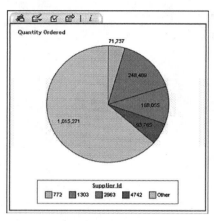

99

Pie Chart – Graph Data

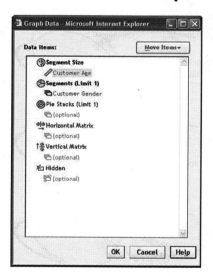

The Graph Data window for a Pie Chart object enables you to select the data item(s) used to represent the following:

- segment size
- number of segments
- pie stacks
- a horizontal or vertical matrix to separate the data in the graph
- hidden data items

100

Pie Chart – Graph Properties

The General tab in the Graph Properties window for a Pie Chart object enables you to select the following:

- title text, font style, size, color, and alignment
- graph size
- background color
- border color
- formatting

101

continued...

Pie Chart – Graph Properties

The Pie tab in the Graph Properties window for a Pie Chart object enables you to select the following:

- pie shape
- multiple measures
- font style, size, and color for labels and values
- show data values
- formatting

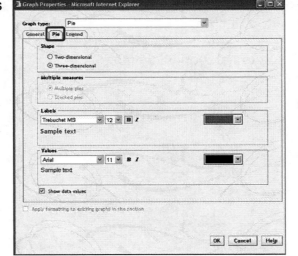

102

continued...

Pie Chart – Graph Properties

The Legend tab in the Graph Properties window for a Pie Chart object enables you to select the following:

- position of the legend
- font style, size, and color for labels
- background color
- formatting

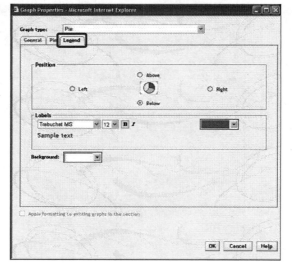

103

Report Objects – Line Graph

A line graph is a graph that shows the relationship of one variable to another, often showing movements or trends in the data over a period of time. Line graphs summarize source data and typically are used to chart response values against discrete categorical values.

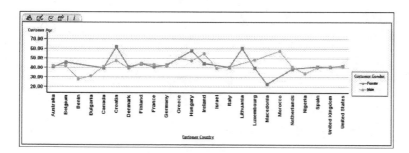

104

Line Graph – Graph Data

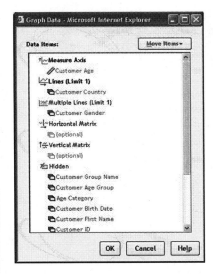

The Graph Data window for a Line Graph object enables you to select the data item(s) used to represent the following:

- measure axis (height of the lines)
- lines (category)
- multiple lines
- a horizontal or vertical matrix to separate the data in the graph
- hidden data items

105

Line Graph – Graph Properties

The General tab in the Graph Properties window for a Line Graph object enables you to select the following:

- title text, font style, size, color, and alignment
- graph size
- background, border, and grid color
- show grid lines
- formatting

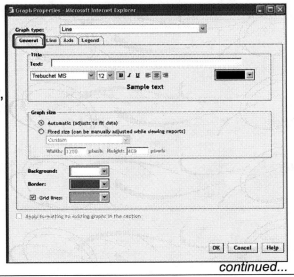

106

continued...

Line Graph – Graph Properties

The Line tab in the Graph Properties window for a Line Graph object enables you to select the following:

- line thickness
- marker size
- show data values
- formatting

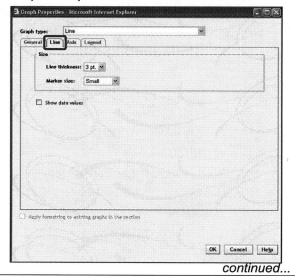

107   continued...

Line Graph – Graph Properties

The Axis tab in the Graph Properties window for a Line Graph object enables you to select the following:

- tick marks
- font style, size, and color for labels and data values
- label orientation
- formatting

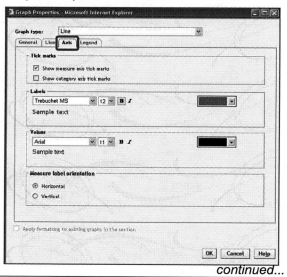

108   continued...

Line Graph – Graph Properties

The Legend tab in the Graph Properties window for a Line Graph object enables you to select the following:

- position of the legend
- font style, size, and color for labels
- background color
- formatting

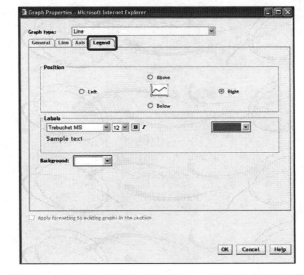

109

Report Objects – Bar-Line Chart

A bar-line chart is a bar chart with an overlaid line graph.

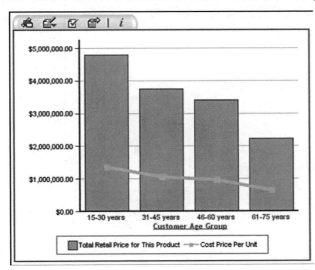

110

Bar-Line Chart – Graph Data

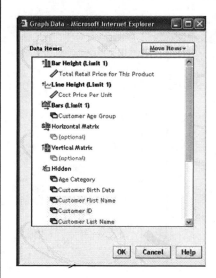

The Graph Data window for a Bar-Line Chart object enables you to select the data item(s) that represent the following:

- bar height
- line height
- number of bars
- a horizontal or vertical matrix to separate the data in the graph
- hidden data items

111

Bar-Line Chart – Graph Properties

The General tab in the Graph Properties window for a Bar-Line Chart object enables you to select the following:

- title text, font style, size, color, and alignment
- graph size
- background, border, and grid color
- show grid lines
- formatting

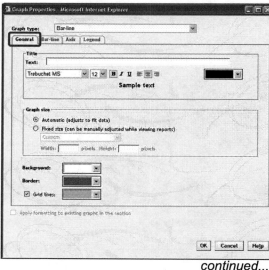

112

continued...

Bar-Line Chart – Graph Properties

The Bar-Line tab in the Graph Properties window for a Bar-Line Chart object enables you to select the following:

- bar shape
- line thickness
- marker size
- bar and line color
- show data values
- formatting

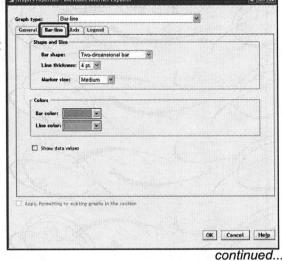

113

continued...

Bar-Line Chart – Graph Properties

The Axis tab in the Graph Properties window for a Bar-Line Chart object enables you to select the following:

- tick marks
- font style, size, and color for labels and data values
- label orientation
- additional axis for second measure
- formatting

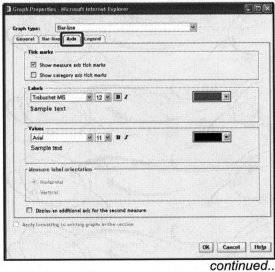

114

continued...

Bar-Line Chart – Graph Properties

The Legend tab in the Graph Properties window for a Bar-Line Chart object enables you to select
the following:

- position of the legend
- font style, size, and color for labels
- background color
- formatting

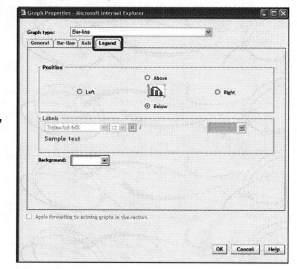

115

Report Objects – Progressive Bar Chart

A progressive bar chart is a type of bar chart that shows how the initial value of a measure data item increases or decreases during a series of operations or transactions.

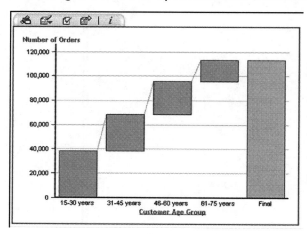

116

Progressive Bar Chart – Graph Data

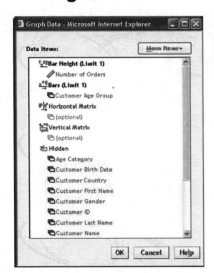

The Graph Data window for a Progressive Bar Chart object enables you to select the data item(s) that represent the following:

- set bar height
- number of bars
- a horizontal or vertical matrix to separate the data in the graph
- hidden data items

117

Progressive Bar Chart – Graph Properties

The General tab in the Graph Properties window for a Progressive Bar
Chart object
enables
you to select the
following:

- title text, font style, size, color, and alignment
- graph size
- background, border, and grid color
- show grid lines
- formatting

118

continued...

Progressive Bar Chart – Graph Properties

The Progressive Bar tab in the Graph Properties window for a Progressive Bar Chart object enables you to select the following:

- set initial bar value and label
- show final value and final bar label
- all bar colors
- show trend line and data values
- formatting

119

continued...

Progressive Bar Chart – Graph Properties

The Axis tab in the Graph Properties window for a Progressive Bar Chart object enables you to select the following:

- tick marks
- font style, size, and color for labels and data values
- label orientation
- formatting

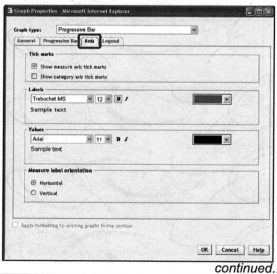

120

continued...

Progressive Bar Chart – Graph Properties

The Legend tab in the Graph Properties window for a
Progressive Bar
Chart object
enables
you to only select
formatting.

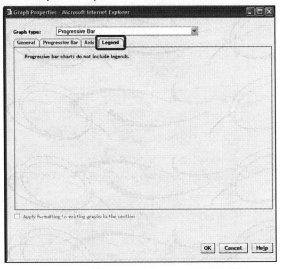

Progressive Bar
Charts do not
include legends.

121

Report Objects – Scatter Plot

A scatter plot is a two- or three-dimensional plot that
shows the crossing of two or three data items.

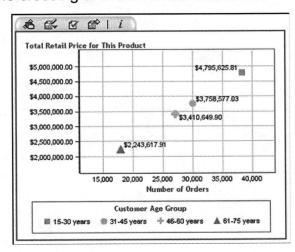

122

Scatter Plot – Graph Data

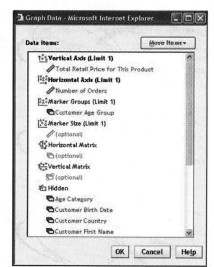

The Graph Data window for a Scatter Plot object enables you to select the data item(s) that represent the following:

- vertical axis
- horizontal axis
- marker groups
- marker size
- a horizontal or vertical matrix to separate the data in the graph
- hidden data items

123

Scatter Plot – Graph Properties

The General tab in the Graph Properties window for a Scatter Plot object enables you to select the following:

- title text, font style, size, color, and alignment
- graph size
- background, border, and grid color
- show grid lines
- formatting

124

continued...

Scatter Plot – Graph Properties

The Markers tab in the Graph Properties window for a Scatter Plot object enables you to select the following:

- marker size
- show data values
- formatting

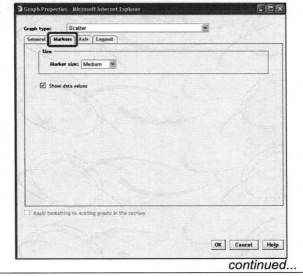

125

continued...

Scatter Plot – Graph Properties

The Axis tab in the Graph Properties window for a Scatter Plot object enables you to select the following:

- tick marks
- font style, size, and color for labels and data values
- label orientation
- formatting

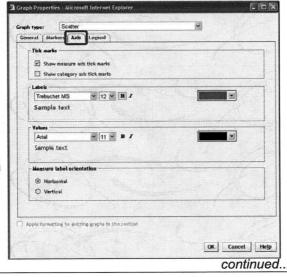

126

continued...

Scatter Plot – Graph Properties

The Legend tab in the Graph Properties window for a Scatter Plot object enables you to select the following:

- position of the legend
- font style, size, and color for labels
- background color
- formatting

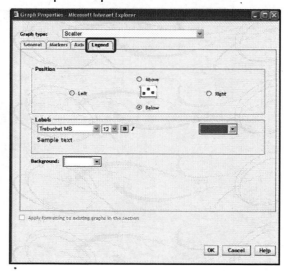

127

Report Objects – Geographical Map

The geographical map object enables you to display your OLAP data in an interactive geographical map.

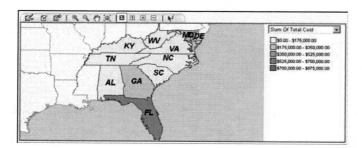

128

Geographical Map – Map Data

The Map Data window for a Geographical Map object
enables you to select the measure to be represented in
the graph.

129

Geographical Map – Edit Map Options

The Filter and Rank window for a Geographical Map
object enables you
to
select the following:

- category filters
  used in the
  graph
- measure filters
  used in the
  graph
- measure
  ranking

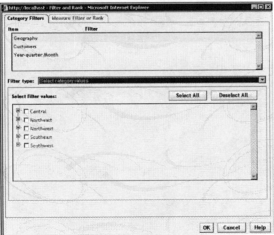

130

Geographical Map – Map Properties

The Map tab in the Map Properties window for a Geographical Map object enables you to select the following:

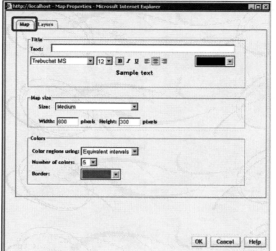

- title text, font style, size, color, and alignment
- map size
- color instructions
- number of colors
- border color

131

continued...

Geographical Map – Map Properties

The Layers tab in the Map Properties window for a Geographical Map object enables you to select the layers to display in the map.

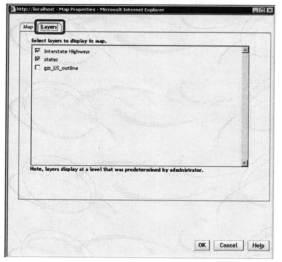

132

Report Objects – Text

Text objects can be used to display static text and can link to another report or a Web page. Text can also be used to display the items selected from dynamic prompt values.

The data in this report has been subset to only show orders for 2002.

Click <u>here</u> to view the Salary Analysis report.

This report is subset by Country - the currently selected values are: Germany France and Spain

133

Text – Edit Text Properties

The Edit Text Properties window enables you to perform the following tasks:

- enter the text to display
- set the text formatting
- specify a link
- insert dynamic values and prompts

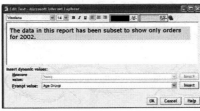

134

Report Objects – Image

Image objects can be used to add static graphics to a report to help identify its use, such as information for the Shoe Division or worldwide sales information.

An Image object can also be set up so that clicking on it links to another report or a Web page.

135

Image – Edit Image Options

The Edit Image Options opens a Select Image window that provides the ability to choose the following:

- an image from the repository or from the local machine
- image size
- text that is displayed when the mouse cursor hovers over the image
- report linking

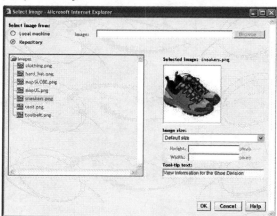

136

Report Objects – Stored Process

A stored process is a SAS program stored on a server that executes and returns results to a report section. Because all of the instructions are part of the stored process, there is only one menu item for the stored process object.

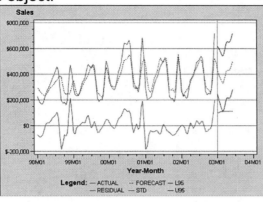

137

Metadata for stored processes must be stored in a specific place in the Metadata server. See Appendix B for more information.

Stored Process – Edit Stored Process

Edit Stored Process opens an Insert Stored Process window that allows you to choose the following:

- location of the stored process (Shared folders or My folders)
- name of the stored process

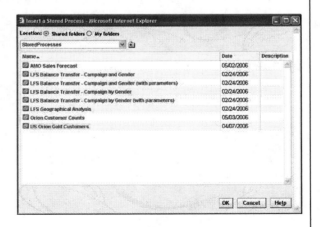

138

4.6   Solutions to Exercises

1. Adding a New Section to the WRS Management Summary Report

  a. Log on to SAS Web Report Studio using the credentials provided by your instructor.

    1) Start Internet Explorer by selecting **Start** ⇨ **Internet**.

    2) Select ⇨ **SAS Web Report Studio**.

    3) Enter the user name and password provided by your instructor and select ⟨ **Log On** ⟩.

  b. Open the WRS Management Summary report created in the demonstration.

    1) Select **Report** ⇨ **Open…** and select **WRS Management Summary**.

      ✎ If you did not follow along with the demonstration, create a new report by selecting **Report** ⇨ **New**.

  c. Use the Edit Report view to modify the report based on the following criteria:

    1) Select ⟨ **Edit Report** ⟩ to toggle to the Edit Report view.

    2) Add a new section to the report.

      a) Select **Section** ⇨ **New…**.

      b) Enter **Salary Information** as the New section name.

      c) Select **Copy header from** and **Employee Counts**.

      d) Select **Copy footer from** and **Employee Counts**.

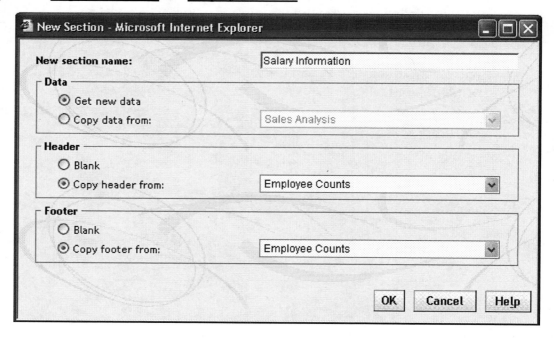

e) Select | OK | to close the New Section window.

3) Select ⨄ to expand the Data area.

a) Select **Select data**.

b) Select | Change Source ... |, select **WRS Organization** and | OK |.

c) Select the following data items:

- **Annual Salary**
- **Company**
- **Employee Country**
- **Employee Gender**

d) Select **Annual Salary** ⇨ | ... ╱ |, enter **Average Annual Salary**, and select | OK |.

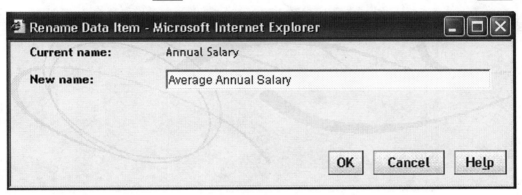

e) Select OK to close the Select Data window.

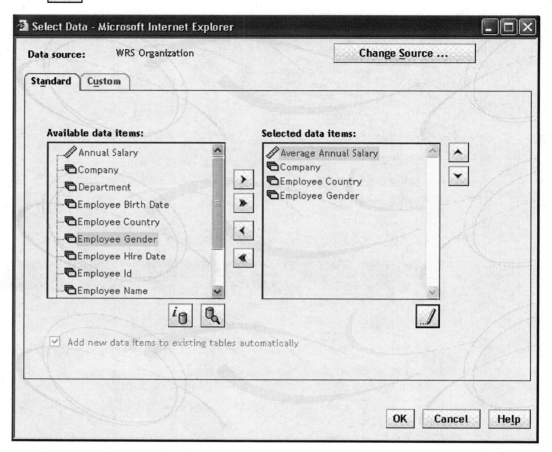

4) Change the default statistic for **Average Annual Salary**.

a) Select **Options** ⇨ **Aggregate or Detail** in the Data area.

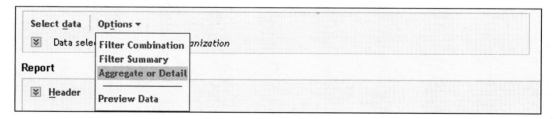

b) Select **Average** from the drop-down list in the `Aggregation` column for **Average Annual Salary**.

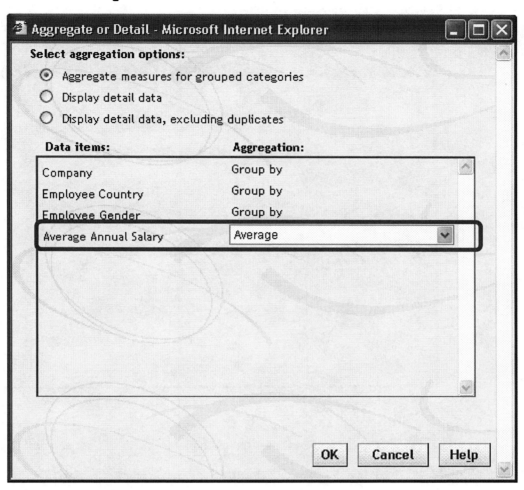

c) Select **OK** to close the Aggregate or Detail window.

d) Select ⊼ to collapse the Data area.

5) Change the Text of the Header.

   a) Select `Header` in the Report area.

   b) Enter **Average Annual Salary Analysis** as the header text.

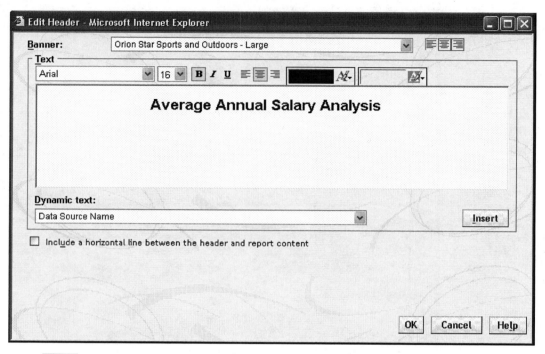

   c) Select **OK** to close the Edit Header window.

6) Add a Bar Chart object and a Line Graph object.

   a) Select 📊 to add a Bar Chart object.

   b) Select 📈 to add a Line Chart object.

   c) Click and drag the line chart under the bar chart.

7) Set the properties for the bar chart.

   a) Select 📦 from the **Graph1** toolbar to specify the Bar Chart data properties.

   b) Select **Employee Country** in the Hidden section.

   c) Select `Move Items▾` ⇨ **Move to Bars**.

   d) Select **Employee Gender** in the Hidden section.

e) Select [**Move Items ▾**] ⇨ **Move to Bar Subgroup**.

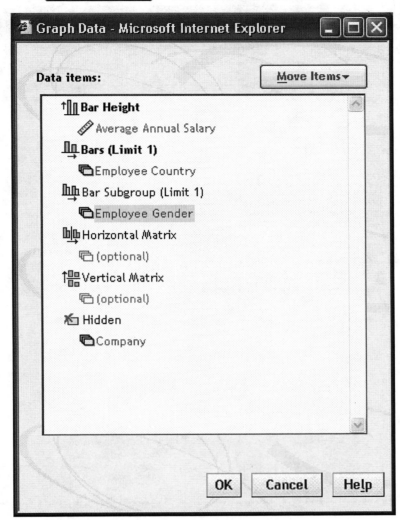

f) Select [**OK**] to close the Graph Data window.

g) On the **Graph1** toolbar, select ☑ to open the Graph Properties window.

h) Select the **Bar** tab.

i) In the Subgroup area, select **Clustered bars**.

j) In the Shape area, select **Three-dimensional cylinder**.

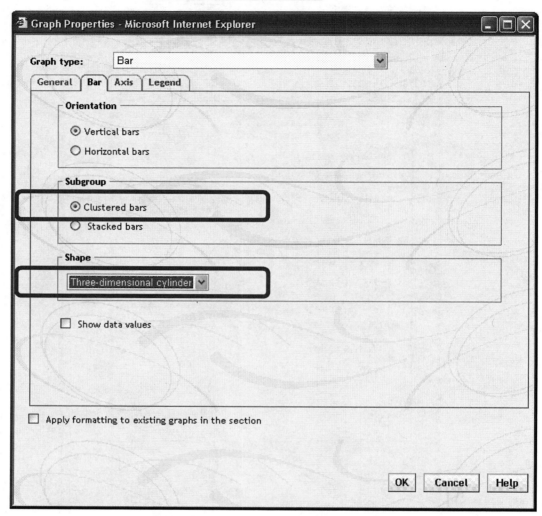

k) Select **OK** to close the Graph Properties window.

8) Set the properties for the line chart.

a) Select 🖆 from the **Graph2** toolbar to specify the Line Chart data properties.

b) Select **Employee Gender** in the Hidden section.

c) Select **Move Items▾** ⇨ **Move to Multiple Lines**.

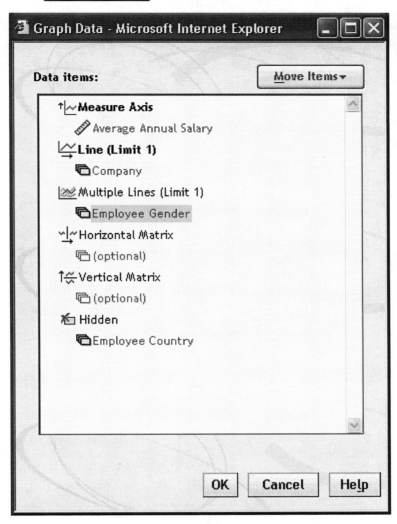

d) Select **OK** to close the Graph Data window.

d. View the report in the View Report view.

1) Select View Report to toggle to the View Report view.

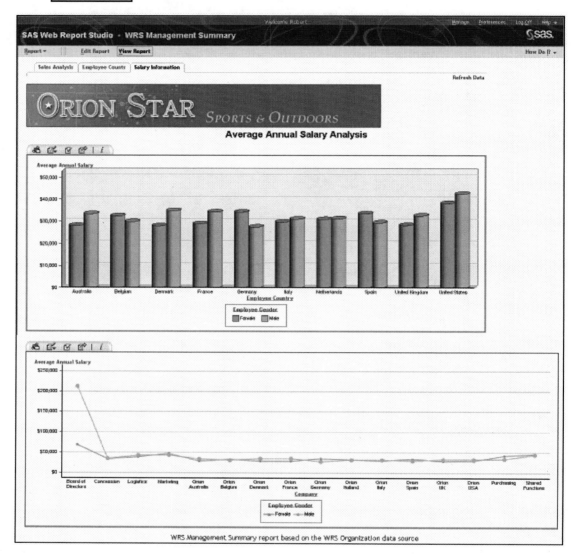

e. Save the report. Replace the previous version by select **Report** ➪ **Save**.

f. Select **Log Off** in the upper-right corner.

2. **Creating a New Synchronized Report**

   a. Log on to SAS Web Report Studio using the credentials provided by your instructor.

   1) Start Internet Explorer by selecting **Start** ⇨ **Internet**.

   2) Select **Favorites** ⇨ **SAS Web Report Studio**.

   3) Enter the user name and password provided by your instructor and select **Log On**.

   b. Select **Report** ⇨ **New** to begin creating a new report using Edit Report view.

   1) Select **Select Data**.

   2) Select **Change Source ...** ⇨ **WRS Product** ⇨ **OK**.

   3) Select **Product Group**, **Supplier Id**, and **Supplier Country**.

   4) Select **Supplier Id** ⇨ [✐] .

   5) Type **Number of Suppliers**.

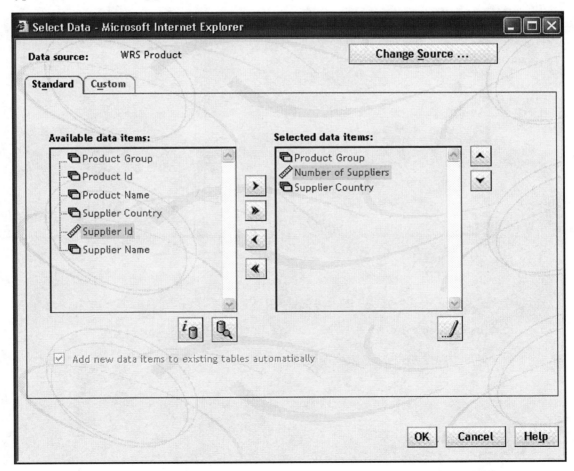

   6) Select **OK**.

7) Select OK to close the Select Data window.

8) Select **Options** ⇨ **Aggregate or Detail**.

9) Change the Aggregation for **Number of Suppliers** to **Count**.

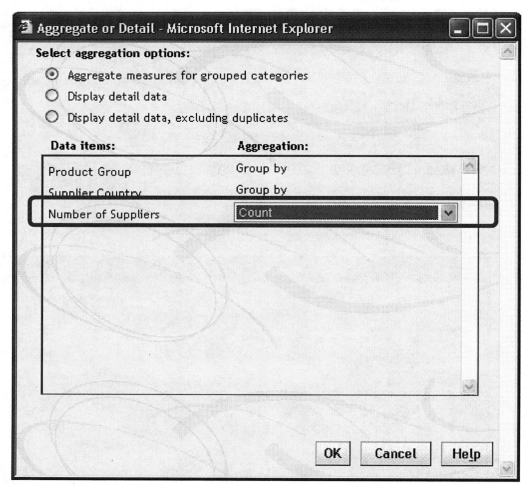

10) Select OK .

c. Select ⌨ to create a filter on **Supplier Country**.

1) Specify values from a list by selecting **Selecting values from a list**.

2) Select **Filter on formatted values**.

3) Select **<u>Canada</u>**, **<u>United Kingdom</u>**, and **<u>United States</u>**.

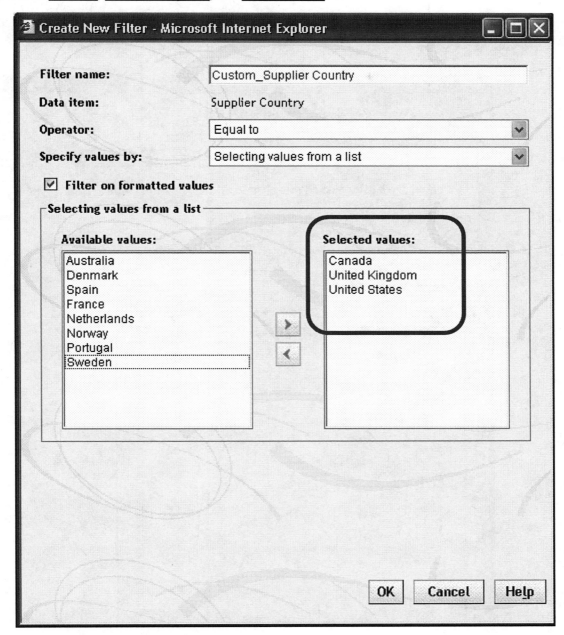

4) Select ` OK `.

d. Add a List object and a Bar Chart object.

1) Select and drag ⊞ to add a List object in the Report area grid.

2) Select and drag 📊 to add a Bar Chart object under the list table object.

e. Synchronize the objects.

1) Select **Synchronized Objects** in the Report Objects toolbar.

2) Select [OK] in the message box.

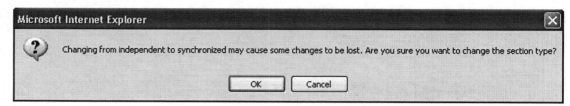

✎   You'll see a gray dashed line around all objects to indicate they are synchronized.

f. Set the properties for the List object.

1) Select 🖫 on the List object to open the Table Data window.

2) Select **Number of Suppliers** ⇨ [Move Items ▾] ⇨ **Move Down**.

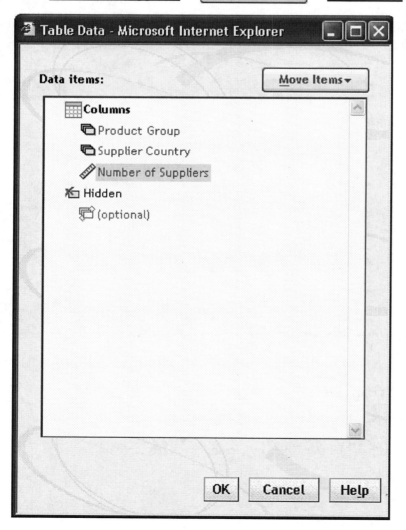

3) Select | **OK** | to close the Table Data window.

g. Set the properties for the Bar Chart object.

1) Select 🏠 on the Bar Chart object to open the Graph Data window.

2) Select **Supplier Country** ⇨ | **Move Items ▾** | ⇨ **Move to Bars**.

3) Select **Product Group** ⇨ | **Move Items ▾** | ⇨ **Move to Bar Subgroup**.

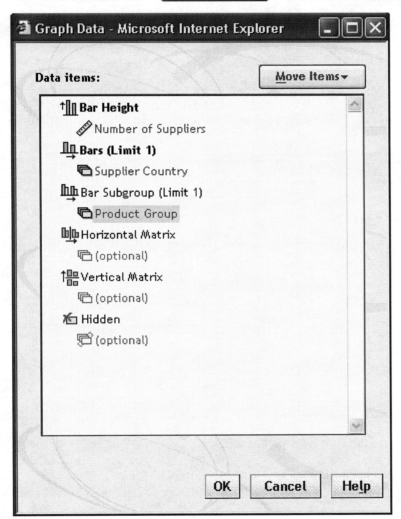

4) Select | **OK** | to close the Graph Data window.

5) Select ☑ on the Bar Chart object toolbar to open the Graph Properties window.

6) Select the **Bar** tab.

7) Select **Horizontal bars**.

8) Select **Three-dimensional bar**.

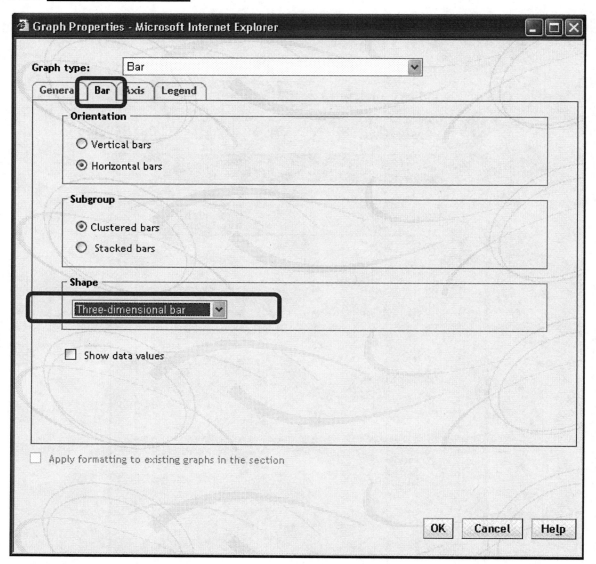

9) Select **OK** to close the Graph Properties window.

h. Enter headers and footers of your choice.

i. Select **View Report** .

1) Select the columns in the table to resize.

2) Select **Supplier Country** ⇨ **Sort Descending**. Notice how the graph is also sorted by descending country since the objects are synchronized.

j. Save the report in `Shared Folders` as **WRS Supplier Count**.

    1) Select **Report** ⇨ **Save As...**.

    2) Enter **WRS Supplier Count** as the `Name`.

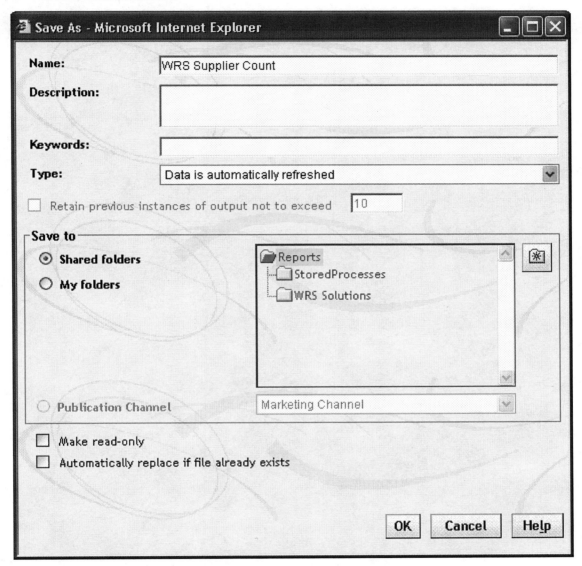

    3) Select **OK** to close the Save As window.

Chapter 5   Interacting with Existing Reports

5.1 Managing Existing Reports

Objectives

- Discuss the options available to search for a report.
- Learn about the various storage locations available.
- Introduce the actions available for existing reports.

3

Managing Reports – Manage Window (Review)

The Manage window allows you to do the following tasks:

- edit
- move, copy, delete, and rename
- print
- export
- schedule
- distribute

4

Interacting with Existing Reports

You can also select **Open ...** from the Report menu, where you have many more choices than just opening an existing report:

- search for a report
- navigate to the various report folders
- create new report folders
- view report descriptions

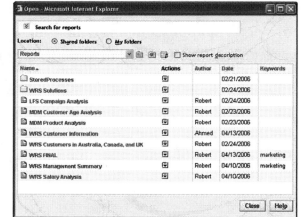

5

Searching for Reports

Selecting 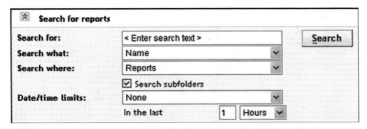 in the Open window expands the search facility, enabling you to search for reports based on the report name, description, and keywords.

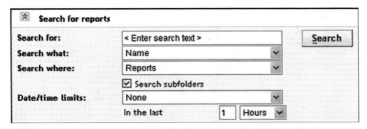

You can also augment the search based on when the report was last modified (hours, days, weeks, or months).

6

Tips for specifying the `Search for` text:

- The search for text is not case sensitive.
- The wildcard character (*) can be used to search for any text.
- If you search for a single word, then SAS Web Report Studio assumes a wildcard character before and after the word.

The `Search where` field allows you to select the folder that you want to search. You can also search folders within the selected folder by selecting the Search subfolders option.

Navigating the Report Folders

When using in the Open window, you can navigate to the **Shared folders** or **My folders** locations. Both locations can contain subfolders to help organize your reports.

The Shared folders location is a public workspace where you can share your reports or access reports shared by others.

The My folders location is your workspace and is not accessible to other users.

7

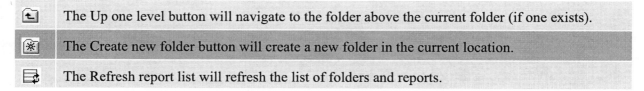

⬆	The Up one level button will navigate to the folder above the current folder (if one exists).
✳	The Create new folder button will create a new folder in the current location.
⬇	The Refresh report list will refresh the list of folders and reports.

✎ SAS Administrators set up permissions to the shared folders and can access your **My Folders** location.

Viewing Report Descriptions

The Open window displays the report name, author, date
(the report was last modified), and keywords. You can
also select **Show report description** to view more
information about each report.

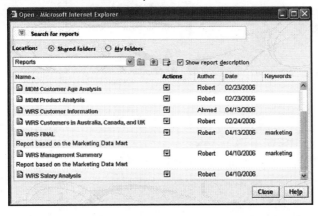

8

Selecting Name, Author, Date, or Keywords will sort the results based on that column.

5.2 Viewing Existing Reports

Objectives

- Explore the report object toolbar.
- Discuss the options available on each report object when viewing an existing report in the View Report view.
- Understand printing and exporting an entire report.
- Schedule a report to run.
- Distribute a report.
- Work with the Report Properties.

10

Report Object Toolbar

Each report object has a toolbar for interacting with the object. There are different toolbars available for the various object types. The toolbar items available are not the same in the Edit Report view and the View Report view.

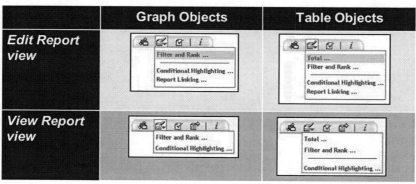

	Graph Objects	Table Objects
Edit Report view	Filter and Rank ... Conditional Highlighting ... Report Linking ...	Total ... Filter and Rank ... Conditional Highlighting ... Report Linking ...
View Report view	Filter and Rank ... Conditional Highlighting ...	Total ... Filter and Rank ... Conditional Highlighting ...

11

Report Object Toolbar

The items on the report object toolbar provide various functionality.

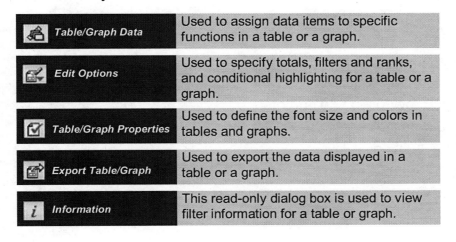

Table/Graph Data	Used to assign data items to specific functions in a table or a graph.
Edit Options	Used to specify totals, filters and ranks, and conditional highlighting for a table or a graph.
Table/Graph Properties	Used to define the font size and colors in tables and graphs.
Export Table/Graph	Used to export the data displayed in a table or a graph.
Information	This read-only dialog box is used to view filter information for a table or graph.

12

Graph Toolbar – View Report View

In the View Report view, the graph toolbar provides the following capabilities:

- specify which data items are used for the various roles by setting the graph data properties
- filter and rank the data in the graph
- set conditional highlighting
- export the data used to build the graph
- display filter information

13

Table Toolbar – View Report View

Total ...

Filter and Rank ...

Conditional Highlighting ...

In the View Report view, the table toolbar provides the following capabilities:

- specify which data items are used for the various roles by setting the table data properties
- turn on column and row totals and subtotals
- filter and rank the data in the table
- set conditional highlighting
- export the data in the table
- display filter information

14

Data Item Roles

When viewing a report you have the ability to change how the data items are used. The same table and graph data windows are available in both Edit Report view and View Report view.

15

Setting Totals

Based on the data selected, you might be able to specify subtotals and totals for both rows and columns.

You might also be able to add new columns that indicate each data value's percentage of the various subtotals and totals.

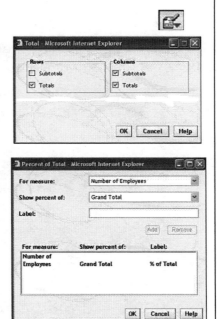

16

Filtering Data

Setting a filter enables you to limit which data is displayed.

Depending on how the data item has been defined in the data source, you might be able to type the values you want or select them from a list of possible values.

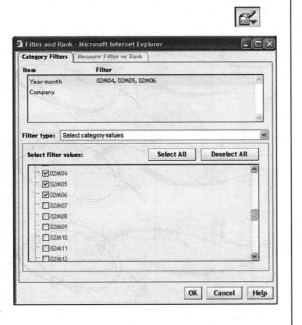

17

Ranking Data

Measures allow you to limit the data displayed
to a specific number or percentage of items.

You can also rank
the rows returned
based on category
values.

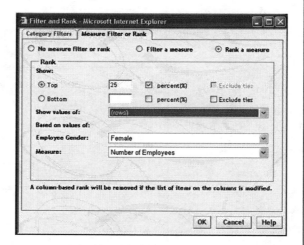

18

Conditional Highlighting

Conditional highlighting can be set on measures to visibly
draw attention to values that meet specific conditions.

Highlighting options
include the following:

- text font, size, and
  style
- cell foreground and
  background colors
- the ability to add an
  image or text in
  addition to or instead
  of the cell value

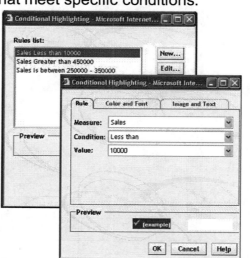

19

Exporting a Report

When viewing a report you can export the data used to build a graph or the data displayed in a table.

Depending on your operating system and browser settings, you are prompted to open or save the export file.

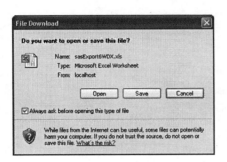

When you export a table you also have the choice to export the data with formats or only the data.

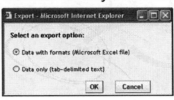

20

You can also export a report on the main SAS Web Report Studio window by selecting **Manage**. Under the Actions menu, select ▼ next to the report name you want to export and select **Export**.

Exporting a Report

When you export the entire report, the zipped file that is created contains the files necessary to display the report in a Web browser or in Microsoft Excel.

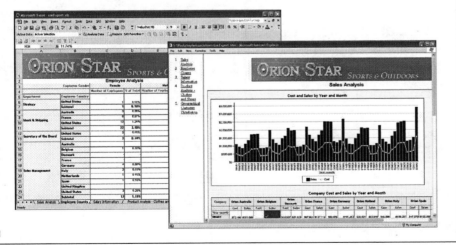

21

Displaying Table or Graph Information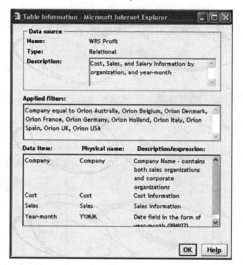

Selecting the information icon on the toolbar opens the
Table or Graph Information
window, which displays
the following:

- data source used
- filters specified in the
  data (including filters
  with user prompts)
- information on how
  multiple filters are
  combined
- descriptions of all
  data items

22

Other Options When Viewing Reports

When viewing a report you can also select the various
data item names in tables and graphs in order to perform
the following functions:

- sorting the data based on the selected data item
- moving the selected data item to another location in
  the table
- rotating a crosstabulation table (swapping the data
  items used to define the columns and rows)

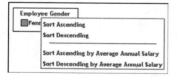 

23

Printing a Report

Under the Report menu, the Page Setup window allows you to specify the following options:

- margins
- page orientation
- paper size
- page numbers

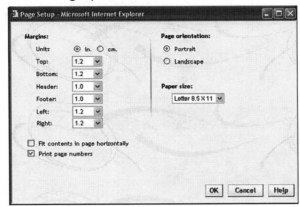

continued...

Printing a Report

The Print window allows you to set the print range and specify if you want page breaks between report sections.

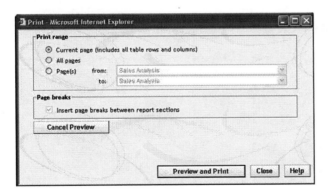

continued...

Printing a Report

Selecting the [**Preview and Print**] button will build a PDF that will open in a new browser window. You can then print or save the report.

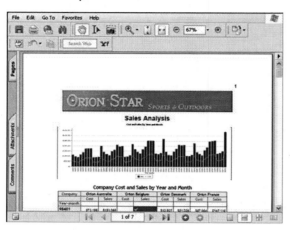

26

✎ You can also print a report on the main SAS Web Report Studio window by selecting **Manage**. Under the Actions menu, select ⊽ next to the report name you want to print and select **Print**.

Scheduling a Report

By selecting **Report** ⇨ **Schedule**, the Schedule Report Wizard opens.

Step 1 enables you to select the following:

- time interval for the report to run
- start time
- start date
- end date
- publication channel

27   *continued...*

✎ A publication channel is an information repository that has been established by using the SAS Publishing Framework. If you publish your report to a publication channel, then authorized users and applications can access your report by subscribing to the channel.

Scheduling a Report

Step 2 of the Schedule Report Wizard enables you to specify the prompt values needed to generate the report.

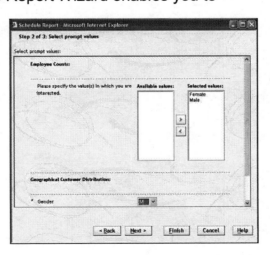

28   *continued...*

✎ You cannot schedule a report that has prompts that do not have default values.

Scheduling a Report

Step 3 of the Schedule Report Wizard summarizes the
report name, time
interval, execution
time, and prompt
values.

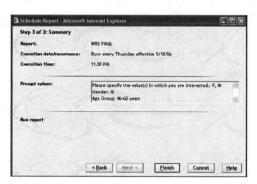

Select Finish to
schedule the report.

29

 You can also schedule a report on the main SAS Web Report Studio window by selecting
Manage. Under the Actions menu, select ▼ next to the report name you want to schedule
and select **Schedule**.

Distributing a Report

Select **Report** ⇨ **Distribute** to open the Distribute Report
Wizard.

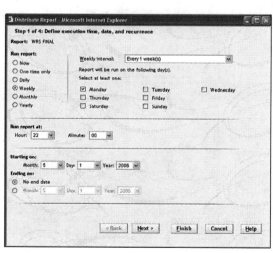

Step 1 of the
Distribute Report
Wizard enables you to
choose the following:

- time interval for
  the report to run
- start time
- start date
- end date

30

continued...

Distributing a Report

Step 2 of the Distribute Report Wizard enables you to specify the prompt values needed to generate the report.

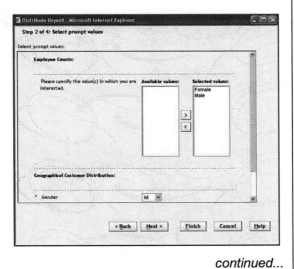

31   *continued...*

You cannot distribute a report that has prompts that do not have default values.

Distributing a Report

Step 3 of the Distribute Report Wizard enables you to specify the following:

- output type (PDF or HTML)
- subject line
- sender's e-mail address
- sender's display name
- message
- recipient rules

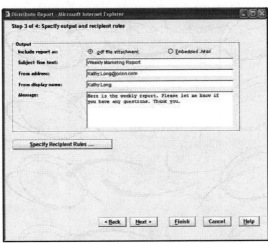

32   *continued...*

Distributing a Report

Select [Specify Recipient Rules ...] to choose the recipients
of the report.

Select [OK] and [Next >]
to move to the next
step.

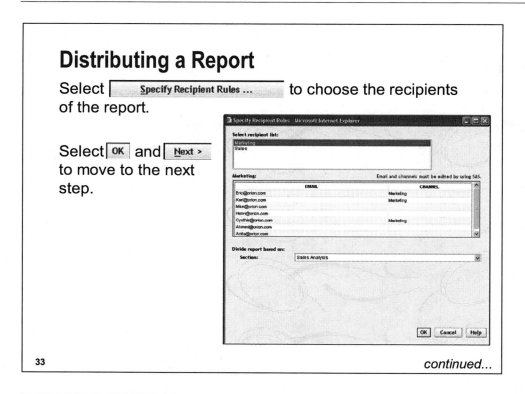

33   *continued...*

Distributing a Report

Step 4 summarizes the report distribution details and
allows you to run a
test and close the
Report Distribution
Wizard.

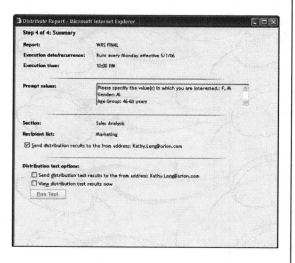

34

You can also distribute a report on the main SAS Web Report Studio window by selecting
Manage. Under the Actions menu, select ▼ next to the report name you want to distribute and
select **Distribute**.

Setting Report Properties

Select **Report** ⇨ **Report Properties**. The General tab in the Report Properties window displays the following:

- report name
- description
- keywords
- creation and modification information

The only modifiable values are description and keywords.

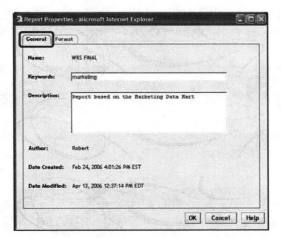

35

continued...

Setting Report Properties

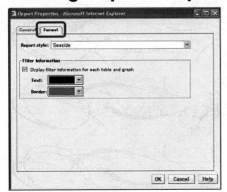

The Format tab in the Report Properties window enables you to choose the following:

- a predefined report style
- the ability to display filter information for each table and graph

Applied Filters: (Year-month equal to 02M01, 02M02, 02M03, 02M04, 02M05, 02M06, 02M07, 02M08, 02M09, 02M10, 02M11, 02M12) AND (Company equal to Orion Australia, Orion Belgium, Orion Denmark, Orion France, Orion Germany, Orion Holland, Orion Italy, Orion Spain, Orion UK, Orion USA)

36

Interacting with Existing Reports

This demonstration shows how to interact with existing reports using the View Report view. Specifically, you filter the report to include only information on or after August, 2002 and display the filter information. You then export the report.

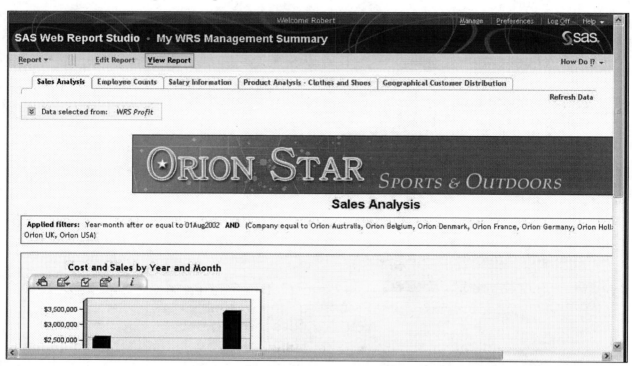

1. If necessary, open a browser window, select **Internet** ⇨ **SAS Web Report Studio**, enter the user name and password provided by your instructor, and select **Log On** .

2. Create a copy of the **WRS Management Summary** report.

   a. Select **Report** ⇨ **Open ...**.

   b. Select the actions button ( ) next to WRS Management Summary.

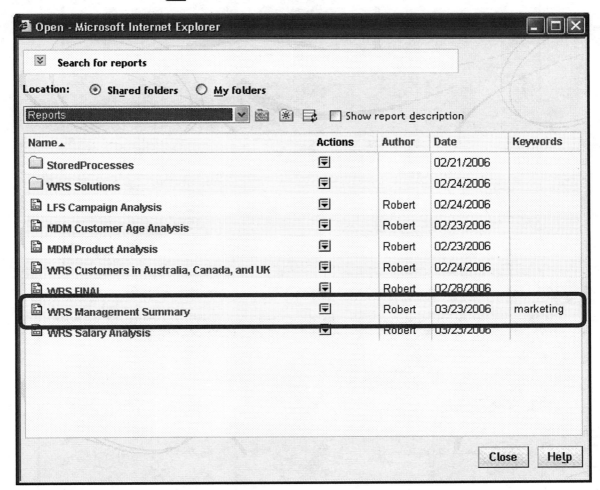

   c. Select **Copy...**.

d.   Copy the report to the My folders location by selecting **My folders** and OK.

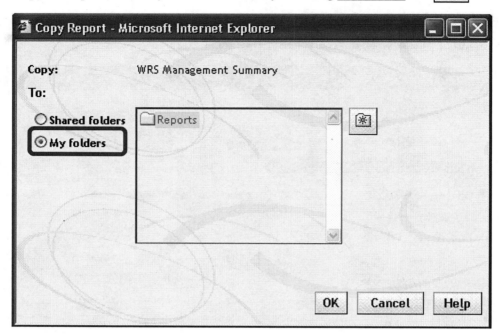

3.   Select **My Folders** in the open dialog box to see the new report.

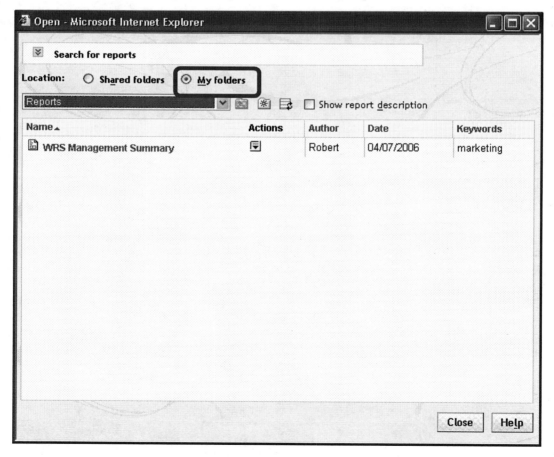

4. Rename the report.

    a. Select the actions button (📋) and select **Rename ...**.

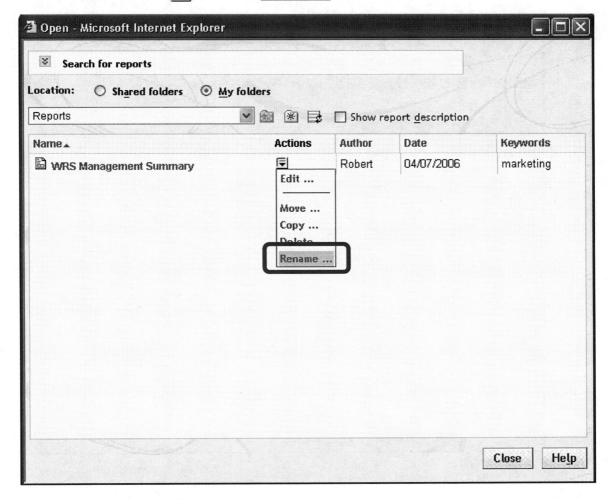

    b. Add **My** at the beginning of the current name.

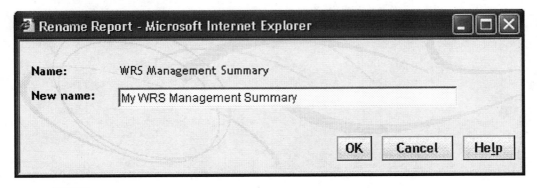

    c. Select OK .

Your renamed report will appear.

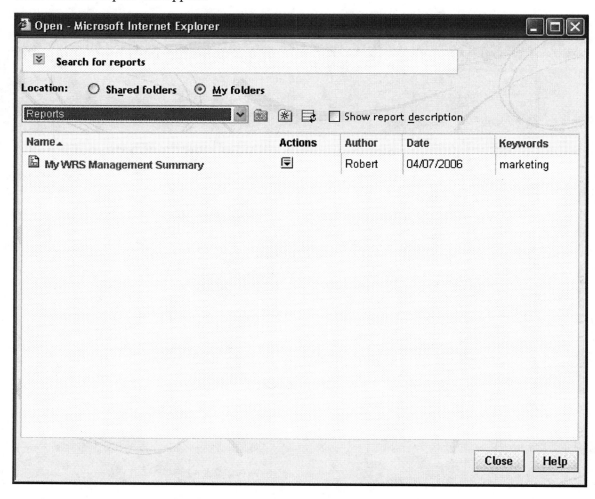

5. Select **My WRS Management Summary** to open the report in View Report view.

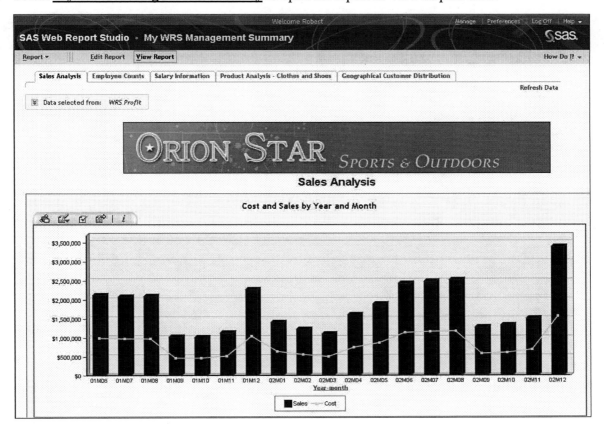

6. Filter the Sales Analysis report section to show only values since August 2002.

    a. Select the edit options button (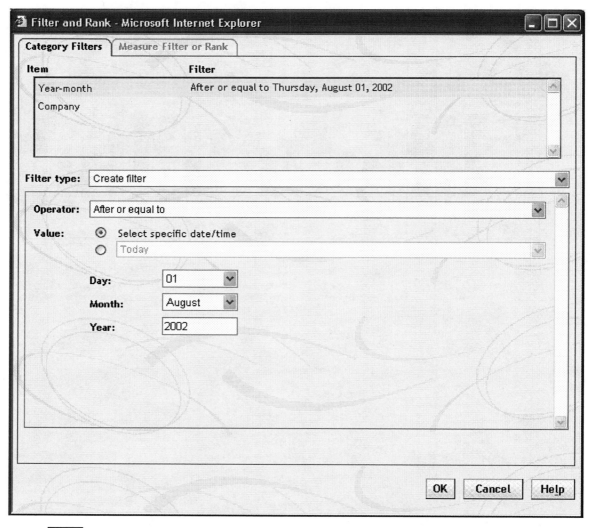) and select **Filter and Rank...**.

    b. Select **Year-month** in the Item area.

    c. Select **Create Filter** for Filter type.

    d. Select **After or equal to** for the Operator.

    e.   Select **Select specific date/time** for the Value.

    f. Select **01** for the Day, **August** for the month, and type in **2002** for the year.

    g. Select **OK** to close the Filter and Rank window.

7. Display filter information on the report.

    a. Select **Report** ⇨ **Report Properties**.

    b. Select the **Format** tab.

    c. Select **Display filter information for each table and graph**.

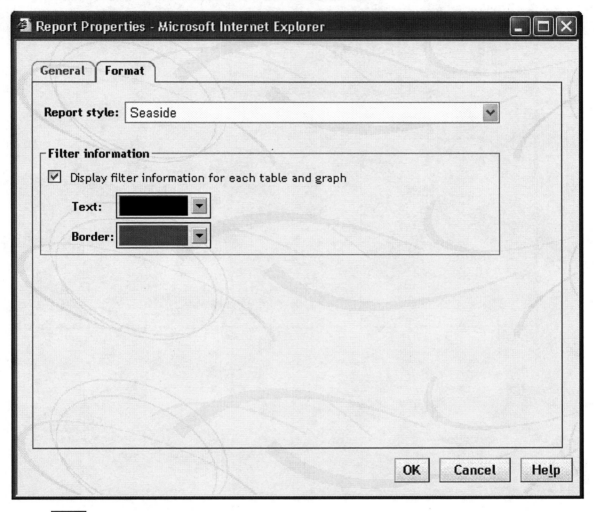

    d. Select **OK** to close the Report Properties window.

8. Preview how the printed report will look.

   a. Select **Report** ⇨ **Print...**.

   b. Select **All pages** and Preview and Print .

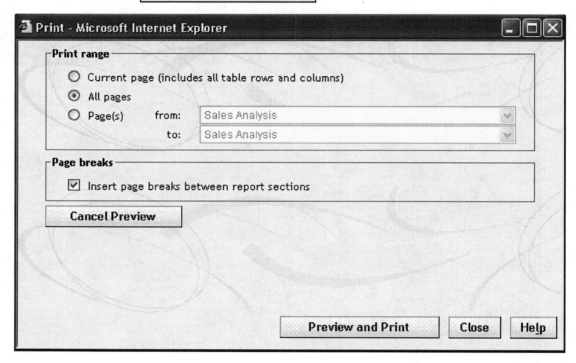

c. Use the scroll bars to view all sections and pages of the report.

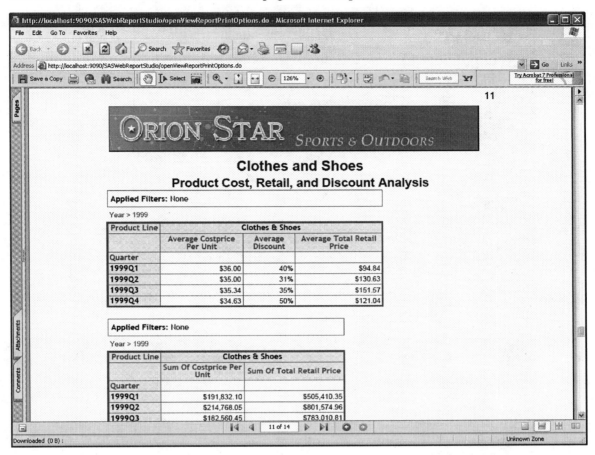

d. After previewing the file, choose 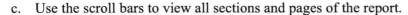 to print the PDF document or ▢ Save a Copy to save a copy of the file.

e. Select **File** ⇨ **Close** to close the Preview window.

f. Select ▢ Close to close the Print window.

9. Export the entire report.

✐ The steps to export and view the export files depends on your browser and operating system settings and may not match what is shown here.

a. Select **Report** ⇨ **Export**.

b. Select [Save].

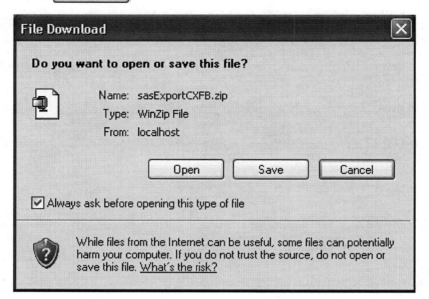

c. Navigate to **S:\Workshop\winsas\sbiwrs** and select [Save].

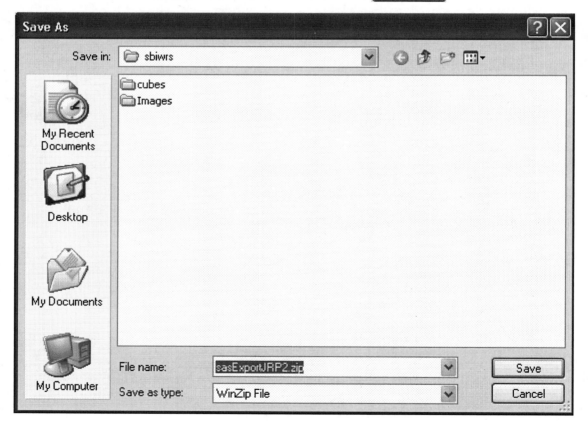

d.   Using the Windows Explorer, navigate to S:\Workshop\winsas\sbiwrs.

e.   Right-click on the new file and select **Winzip** ⇨ **Extract to folder S:\Workshop\winsas\sbiwrs\sasExport*xxxx*** (where *xxxx* is part of the automatically generated name).

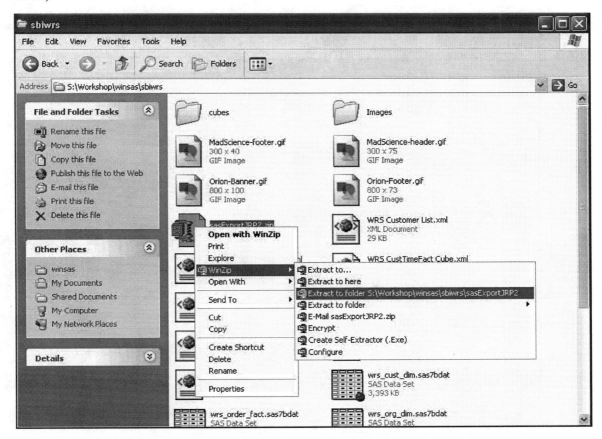

f.   Double-click the new **sasExport** folder.

g.   Double-click the file **sasExport.html**.

h. Use the links in the left window to view each report section.

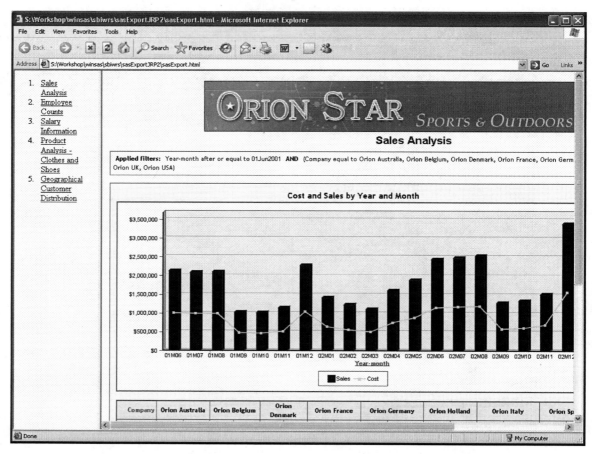

i. Select **File** ⇨ **Close** to close the browser window.

j. Select **File** ⇨ **Close** to close any Windows Explorer windows.

10. Exit SAS Web Report Studio.

a. Select **Log off** in the upper-right corner.

b. Select OK when prompted about not saving the report.

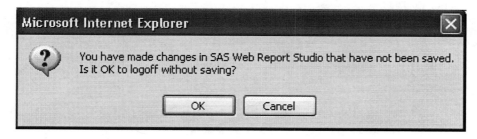

Chapter 6 SAS Reports and the SAS Information Delivery Portal (Self-Study)

6.1 Overview of the SAS Information Delivery Portal

Objectives

- Understand the purpose of the SAS Information Delivery Portal.
- Explore the components of the SAS Information Delivery Portal.

3

SAS Information Delivery Portal

The SAS Information Delivery Portal provides an interface to access enterprise data, applications, and information.

SAS Information Delivery Portal has the following characteristics:

- it is built on top of the SAS Intelligence Platform
- it provides a single point of access for many of the items that can be developed with SAS Intelligence Platform applications
- it provides a Portal API for application development

4

SAS Information Delivery Portal

The SAS Information Delivery Portal has many features, including the following:

> The portal's personalization features enable you to organize your portal desktop so that it contains only the information you need, in the format that makes the most sense to you.

> The ability to subscribe to publication channels that deliver continually updated information to your desktop.

> A secure environment for sharing information with other users.

5

SAS Information Delivery Portal

The SAS Information Delivery Portal uses pages and portlets to organize information.

> A **page** is a Web page in the SAS Information Delivery Portal that contains portlets. Each page is represented by a tab on the portal's navigation bar.

> **Portlets** are the rectangular components on a portal page and are used to organize content.

6

SAS Information Delivery Portal

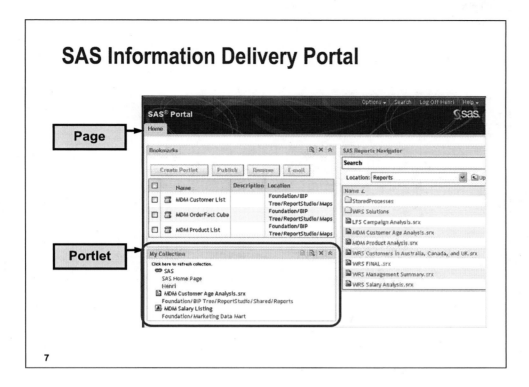

7

Personalizing Your Portal

When you log on to the portal, your personal portal appears. You can modify this view of the portal according to your individual preferences and need for information.

When you make these modifications, you are *personalizing* the portal.

8

6.2 Accessing Reports in the SAS Information Delivery Portal

Objectives

- Learn how to access SAS Web Report Studio reports in the SAS Information Delivery Portal.

10

Using the SAS Information Delivery Portal

When you first connect to the SAS Information Delivery Portal you are at the Public Kiosk. This is a public area of the portal that does not require you to log on.

To access the full power of the portal, you must log on.

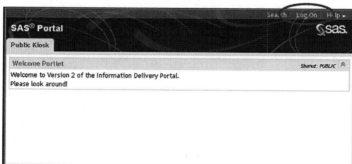

11   ...

Using the SAS Information Delivery Portal

After logging on, your personalized portal is displayed.
The initial view of the portal contains content set up by the
portal administrator or a default page with two portlets.

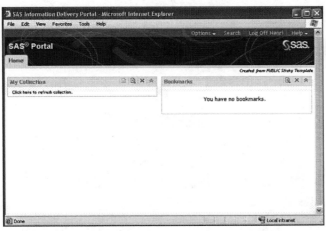

12

Using the SAS Information Delivery Portal

While in the portal, you have many choices to customize
your portal content.

You can perform the following tasks:
- add new pages
- add portlets to existing pages
- modify or remove existing portlets and/or pages
- search for content

13

Using the SAS Information Delivery Portal

To interact with SAS Web Report Studio reports in the portal, choose among these:

- select reports that you have added to your collection portlet
- use the Reports Navigator portlet
- search for content

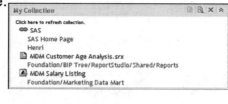

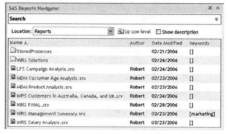

14

Using the SAS Information Delivery Portal

Select the name of the report that you want to work with, which opens the report in the SAS Web Report Viewer. The SAS Web Report Viewer has similar functionality as the View Report view of SAS Web Report Studio.

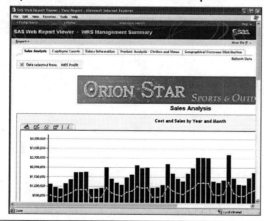

15

Using the SAS Information Delivery Portal

1. Start Internet Explorer by selecting **Start** ⇨ **Internet**.

2. Select **Favorites** ⇨ **SAS Information Delivery Portal**.

> 🖉 You can also enter this URL (Web address) to access SAS Information Delivery Portal.
> (This URL is valid only on the classroom machine and is case sensitive.)
>
> `http://localhost:9090/Portal`

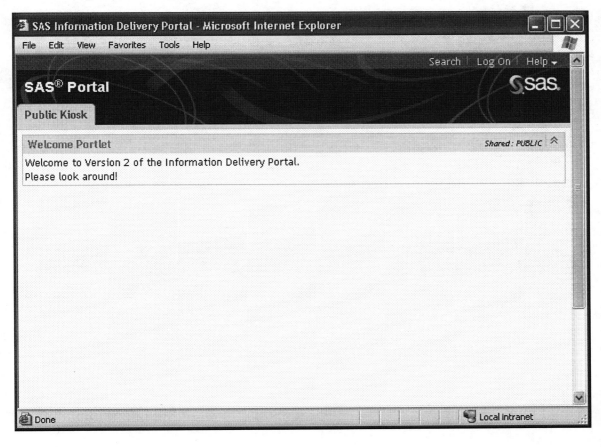

3. Select [Log On] in the upper-right corner.

4. Enter the user name and password provided by your instructor.

5. Select [Log On].

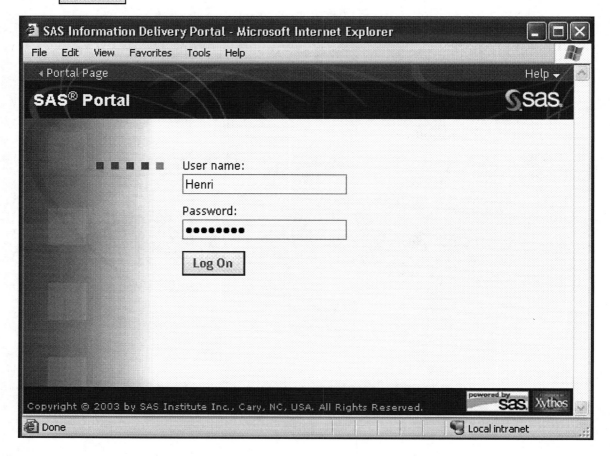

The portal displays the initial start-up page.

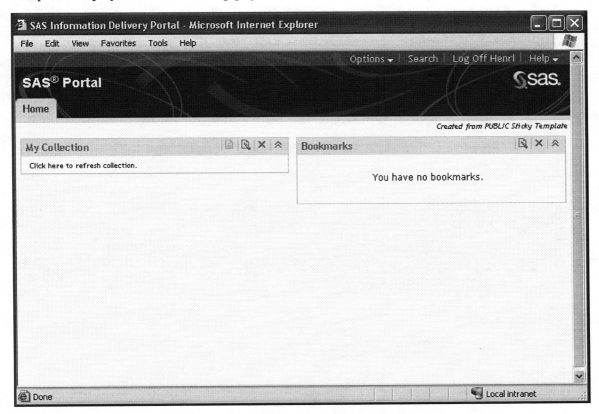

This is the portal default, which has not been customized for this user.

Search for All Available Reports

1. Begin by searching for available reports.

   a. Select **Search** in the upper-right corner.

   b. Enter an asterisk (*****) in the Keywords field.

   ✐   The asterisk is a wild card that allows you to search for all content.

   c. Select the check box for **SAS Report**, which will search for reports only.

   d. Select Search .

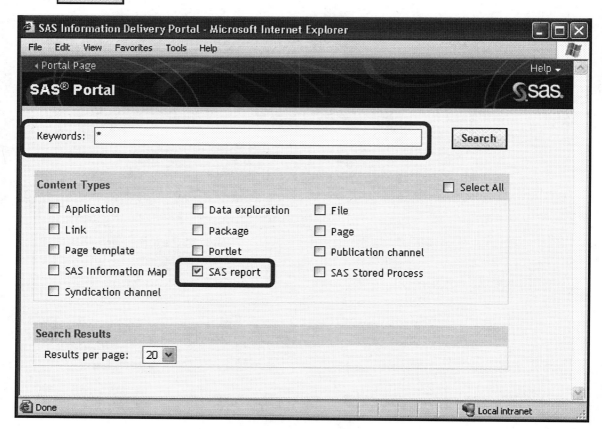

e. When the search results are displayed, select **WRS Management Summary.srx** to open that report.

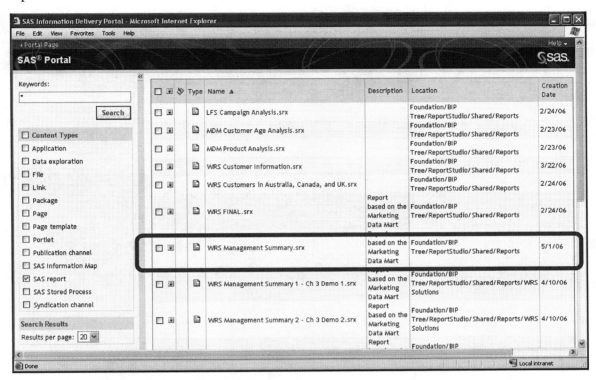

2. The report opens in SAS Web Report Viewer, which provides similar functionality to the View Report view in SAS Web Report Studio.

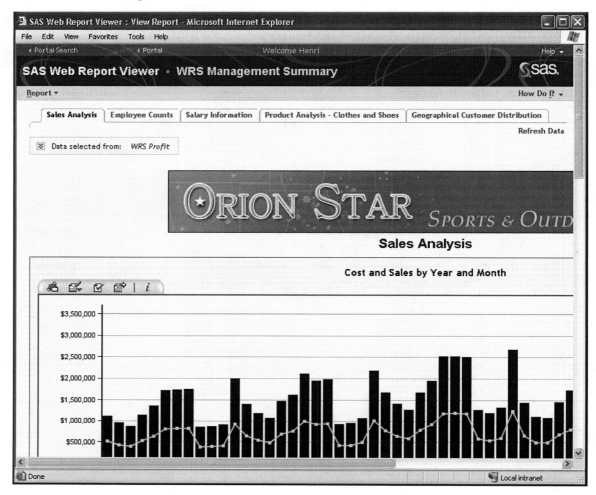

3. Select **Portal** in the upper-left corner to return to the original portal page.

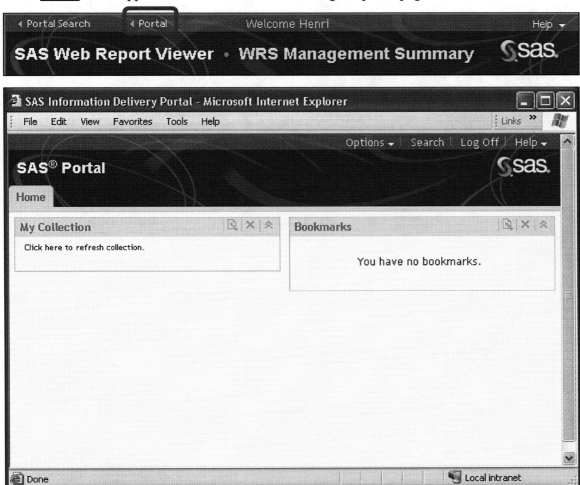

4. Add the Reports Navigator portlet to the Home page.

   a. Select **Options** ⇨ **Edit Content…**.

   b. Select **Add Portlets…**.

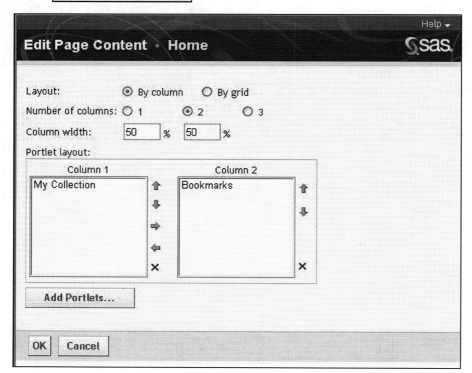

   c. Select the **Search** tab.

   d. Enter an asterisk (*****) in the Keywords field and select **Search**.

e. Select the check box next to SAS Reports Navigator.

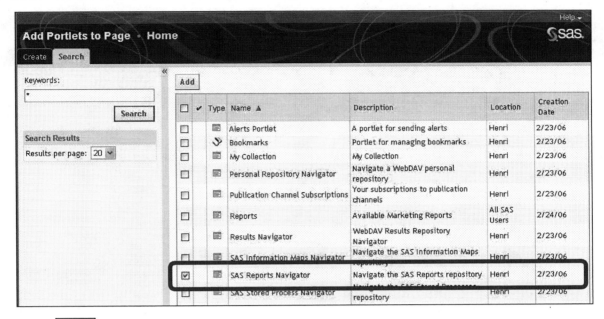

f. Select **Add** .

g. Scroll to the bottom of the window and select **Done** (in the lower-left corner).

h. Select **OK** .

i. The Home page is displayed and now contains the Reports Navigator portlet.

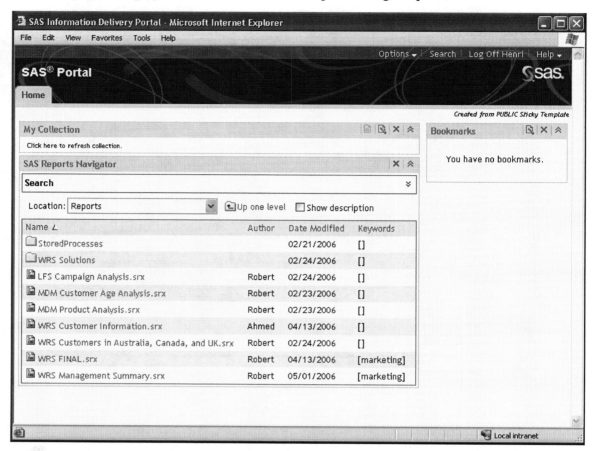

5. Search for reports that contain the keyword marketing.

a. Select ⨆ in the Search section of the SAS Reports Navigator to expand the search selection area.

b. Type **marketing** in the Search for box.

c. Select **Keywords** in the Search what box.

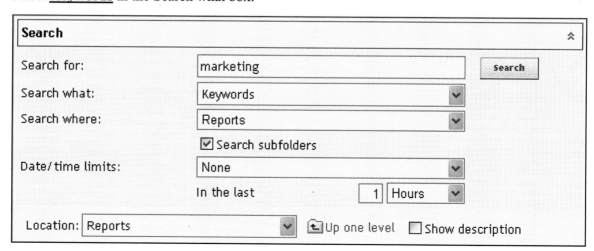

d. Select Search .

e. The results of the search are displayed in the SAS Reports Navigator portlet.

Name ∠	Author	Date Modified	Keywords	Path
WRS Management Summary.srx	Robert	03/23/2006	[marketing]	SBIP://Foundation/BIP Tree/ReportStudio/Shared/Reports/WRS Management Summary.srx(Report)
WRS Management Summary.srx	Robert	04/07/2006	[marketing]	SBIP://Foundation/BIP Tree/ReportStudio/Shared/Reports/WRS Solutions/WRS Management Summary.srx(Report)
WRS Management Summary – Ch 3 Demo 1.srx	Robert	04/06/2006	[marketing]	SBIP://Foundation/BIP Tree/ReportStudio/Shared/Reports/WRS Solutions/WRS Management Summary – Ch 3 Demo 1.srx(Report)
WRS Management Summary – Ch 3 Demo 2.srx	Robert	04/06/2006	[marketing]	SBIP://Foundation/BIP Tree/ReportStudio/Shared/Reports/WRS Solutions/WRS Management Summary – Ch 3 Demo 2.srx(Report)
WRS Management Summary – Ch 4 Demo 1.srx	Robert	04/07/2006	[marketing]	SBIP://Foundation/BIP Tree/ReportStudio/Shared/Reports/WRS Solutions/WRS Management Summary – Ch 4 Demo 1.srx(Report)

f. Select **Reports** in the SAS Reports Navigator to return to the list of shared reports.

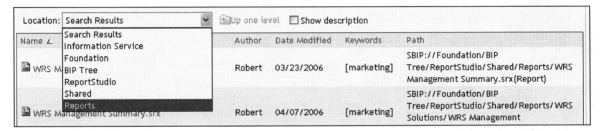

6. Exit the portal.

a. Select **Log Off Henri** in the upper-right corner.

b. Select **File** ⇨ **Close** to close the browser window.

Exercises

1. View the WRS Customers in Australia, Canada, and UK report.

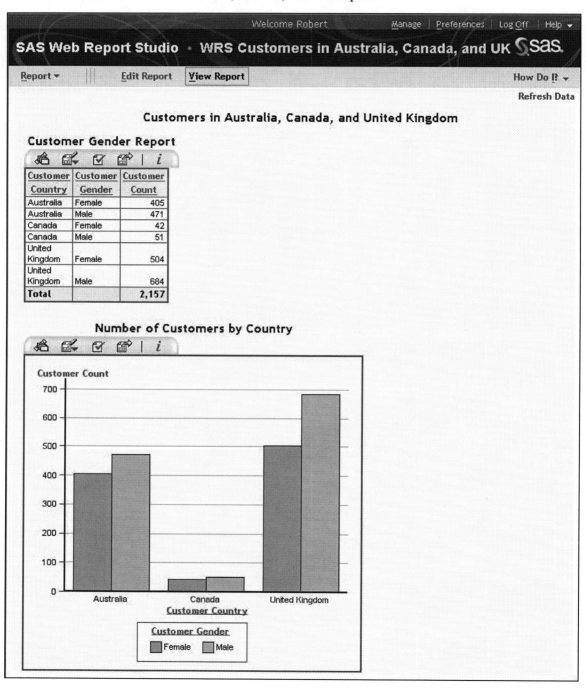

2. (Optional) Add the WRS Customers in Australia, Canada, and UK report to the My Collection portlet.

Hint: Use the Edit Content button (▨) to add items to the My Collection portlet.

6.3 Solutions to Exercises

1. View the WRS Customers in Australia, Canada, and UK report.

    a. Start Internet Explorer by selecting **Start** ⇨ **Internet**.

    b. Select **Favorites** ⇨ **SAS Information Delivery Portal**.

    > 🖊 You can also enter this URL to access SAS Information Delivery Portal. (This URL is only valid on the classroom machine and is case sensitive.)

    > `http://localhost:9090/Portal`

    c. Enter the user name and password provided by your instructor and select `Log On`.

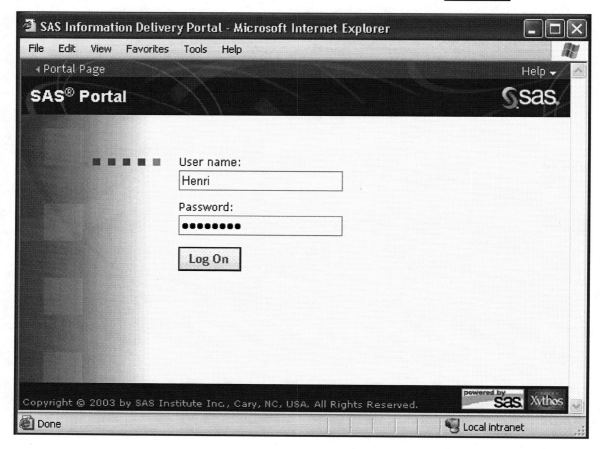

d. Search for the WRS Customers in Australia, Canada, and UK report.

    1) Select ⟱ in the Search section of the SAS Reports Navigator to expand the search selection area.

    2) Type **Australia** in the Search for box.

    3) Select **Name** in the Search what box.

    4) Select [Search].

Search		⟰
Search for:	Australia	[Search]
Search what:	Name ▾	
Search where:	Reports ▾	
	☑ Search subfolders	
Date/time limits:	None ▾	
	In the last	1 Hours ▾
Location: Reports ▾	⤴ Up one level ☐ Show description	

e. Select **WRS Customers in Australia, Canada, and UK** to view the report.

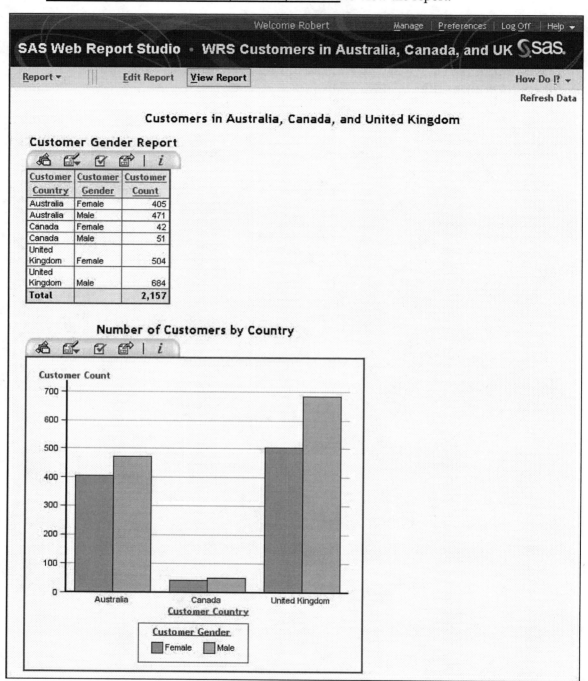

f. Select **Portal** in the upper-left corner to return to the Home page.

2. (Optional) Add the WRS Customers in Australia, Canada, and UK report to the My Collection portlet.

    a. Select the Edit Content button (⬚) to add items to the My Collection portlet.

    b. Select   **Add Items...** .

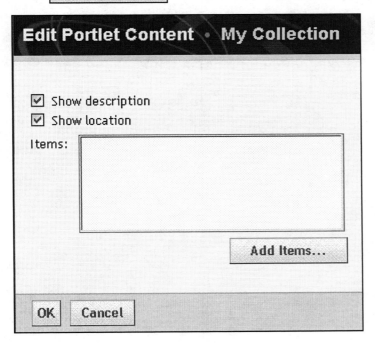

c. Select the **Search** tab.

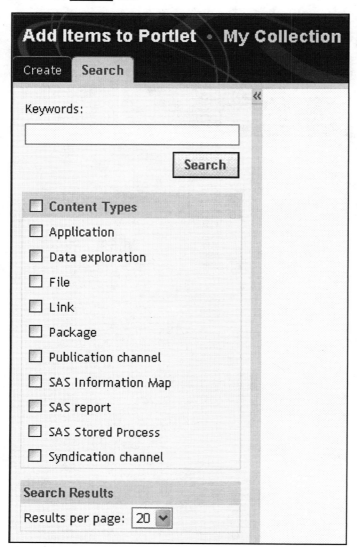

d. Type **Customers** as the keyword, select the check box for **SAS Report**, and select Search .

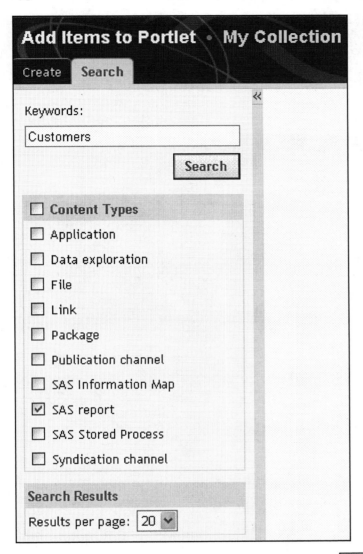

e. Select the check box next to the report name and select Add .

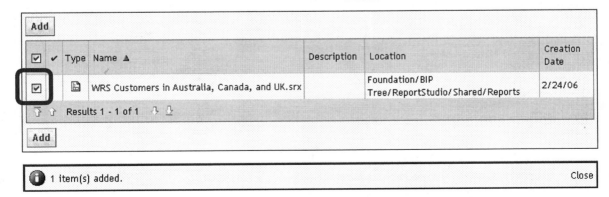

f. Select Done (in the lower-left corner) to return to the Edit Portlet Content screen.

g. Select OK to return to the Home page.

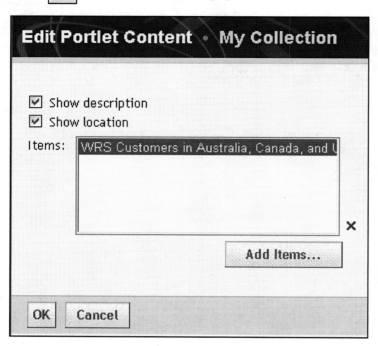

h. The My Collection portlet now contains the WRS Customers in Australia, Canada, and UK report.

i. Exit the portal.

1) Select **Log Off Henri** in the upper-right corner.

2) Select **File** ⇨ **Close** to close the browser window.

Appendix A SAS Intelligence Platform Training

A.1 SAS Intelligence Platform Training

SAS Intelligence Platform – Instructor-Based Training

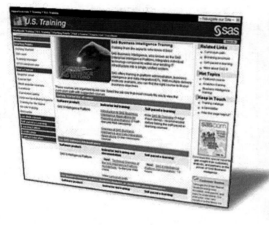 

http://support.sas.com/training/bi/

2

SAS Intelligence Platform – Instructor-Based Training: Getting Started

The courses in this path are intended as a starting point to provide an overview of the SAS Intelligence Platform.

| Introduction to SAS® Business Intelligence Applications for Reporting and Analysis | **or** | Overview of SAS® Business Intelligence and Data Integration Applications |

■ Classroom
▨ Live Web

3

Introduction to SAS® Business Intelligence Applications for Reporting and Analysis

Audience   This Level I course is designed for anyone who wants a hands-on introduction to several of the SAS business intelligence applications. The course requires the SAS Intelligence Platform.

Course   This course provides a hands-on overview of the features and functionality available in
Description   the applications of the SAS Intelligence Platform. You work with the SAS Add-In for Microsoft Office, SAS Web Report Studio, SAS Enterprise Guide, SAS Information Map Studio, and SAS Management Console.

Prerequisites   No SAS experience or programming experience is required, although you should

- have some computer experience. Specifically, you should be able to log on and off a computer and use a keyboard or mouse.

- have some experience using Microsoft Word and Microsoft Excel. Specifically, you should be able to open and save documents, use the menus and toolbars to accomplish tasks, and navigate Word documents and Excel spreadsheets.

- know how to use a Web browser to access information.

Duration   3 half-day sessions

Overview of SAS® Business Intelligence and Data Integration Applications

Audience   This Level II course is designed for anyone who wants a comprehensive, hands-on overview of the SAS business intelligence and data integration applications. The course requires the SAS Intelligence Platform.

Course   This course provides a hands-on overview of the features and functionality available in
Description   the applications of the SAS Intelligence Platform. You work with the SAS Management Console, SAS Data Integration Studio, SAS OLAP Cube Studio, and SAS Information Map Studio to build a data mart. The information in the data mart is analyzed and reported on using SAS Enterprise Guide, the SAS Add-In for Microsoft Office, SAS Web Report Studio, and the SAS Information Delivery Portal.

Prerequisites   No SAS experience or programming experience is required although you should

- have some computer experience. Specifically, you should be able to log on and off a computer and use a keyboard or mouse.

- have some experience using Microsoft Office applications. Specifically, you should be able to open and save documents, use the menus and toolbars to accomplish tasks, and navigate Word documents, PowerPoint presentations, and Excel spreadsheets.

- know how to use a Web browser to access information.

Duration   2 days

SAS Intelligence Platform – Instructor-Based Training: Platform Administration Training

The courses in this path are intended for the people who will install, configure, and administer the SAS Intelligence Platform.

NEW!

Technical Overview of
the SAS® Intelligence
Platform Architecture

NEW!

Introduction to Metadata
Security Using SAS®9

4   ☑ Live Web

Technical Overview of the SAS® Intelligence Platform Architecture

Audience	This Level IV self-paced e-learning library is for information technology professionals with little or no SAS experience who are responsible for administering the SAS®9 Intelligence Platform.
Course Description	This self-paced e-learning prepares administrators to maintain, extend, and administer the SAS Business Intelligence system. The training addresses fundamentals of the architecture for the SAS Intelligence Platform, data access, and user maintenance.
Prerequisites	There are no formal prerequisites. Before taking this e-learning, you should have experience supporting operating systems and administering the user environment. It is also suggested that you view the free SAS Business Intelligence Overview e-learning tutorial before completing this e-learning module.
Duration	Self-paced, approximately 13 hours

Introduction to Metadata Security Using SAS®9

Audience	This course is designed for those who will be involved in administering the servers and applications in the SAS Intelligence architecture.
Course Description	This course focuses on the following key areas: authentication, authorization, metadata permissions, securing metadata objects, metadata users and groups, securing your metadata.
Prerequisites	Before attending this course, you should • read the SAS Intelligence Platform: Overview (.pdf) • attend or be familiar with the content of the Technical Overview of the SAS Intelligence Platform Architecture Live Web class • become familiar with which SAS Intelligence Platform components are installed and configured at your site.
Duration	3 half-day sessions

SAS Intelligence Platform – Instructor-Based Training: Data Integration and ETL Training

The courses in this path are intended for data warehouse architects and others who are responsible for collecting, cleansing, and storing data so that it can be used by business analysts and decision makers for reporting and analysis.

Using SAS® Data Integration Studio to Build Data Marts from Enterprise Data Sources	Using the SAS® Data Quality Solution to Cleanse Your Data
Creating and Exploiting OLAP Using the SAS® System	Using the SAS® Scalable Performance Data Server

5

■ Classroom

Using SAS® Data Integration Studio to Build Data Marts from Enterprise Data Sources

Audience	This Level III course is for data warehouse project leaders, ETL designers, systems experts, and/or data modelers who will be involved in the extraction, transformation, and loading of data into a warehouse. This course requires the SAS Intelligence Platform.
Course Description	This course provides an overview of SAS Data Integration Studio, formerly known as SAS ETL Studio. You learn how to navigate through the SAS Data Integration Studio interface and how to extract, transform, and load data using SAS Data Integration Studio. Additional topics include how to use SAS Data Integration Studio plug-ins and data warehouse management such as change management, scheduling, and use of metadata.
Prerequisites	Before attending this course, you should be familiar with

- the SAS programming language

- Structured Query Language (SQL)

- data modeling concepts.

You can obtain the SAS programming knowledge by completing the SAS Programming I: Essentials course and the SQL knowledge by attending the SQL Processing with SAS course.

Duration	3 days

Using the SAS® Data Quality Solution to Cleanse Your Data

Audience	This Level III course is designed for data quality analysts, warehouse consultants, and ETL specialists who want to learn the tools and techniques of using DataFlux dfPower Studio and the SAS Data Quality Solution to cleanse data. This course requires the SAS Intelligence Platform, as well as DataFlux dfPower Studio.
Course Description	This course introduces you to the issues relating to data quality and provides hands-on experience using DataFlux dfPower Studio, SAS Data Integration Studio (formerly known as SAS ETL Studio), and the SAS Data Quality Solution. You gain an understanding of the essentials of data quality and gain specific knowledge of data profiling and analysis, standardization and scheme building, duplicate elimination and match code generation, and data augmentation and enhancement.
Prerequisites	Knowledge of data cleansing issues, SAS programming, and SAS Data Integration Studio is helpful but not required.
Duration	2 days

Creating and Exploiting OLAP Using the SAS® System

Audience	This Level II course is designed for data modelers and system experts who want to understand, create, and exploit Online Analytical Processing (OLAP) using SAS. This course requires the SAS Intelligence Platform.
Course Description	This course defines SAS OLAP cubes and explores their characteristics. This course also demonstrates how to create and exploit SAS OLAP cubes using a variety of SAS products, including SAS OLAP Cube Studio, SAS Enterprise Guide, SAS Information Delivery Portal, SAS Web OLAP Viewer for Java, and Microsoft Excel with the SAS OLAP Data Provider.
Prerequisites	Familiarity with SAS programming and table structures is helpful but not required. You can gain SAS knowledge by completing the SAS Programming I: Essentials course. Familiarity with Structured Query Language (SQL) or Multidimensional eXpressions (MDX) is also helpful, but not required.
Duration	2 days

Using the SAS® Scalable Performance Data Server

Audience	This Level IV course is designed for SAS programmers, UNIX or Windows administrators, and administrators of the Scalable Performance Data Server in the Windows or UNIX operating environments.
Course Description	This course provides an overview of SPD Server architecture and data and index storage in the SPD Server. This course also covers installing SPD Server, using SPD Server SQL Pass-Through, and optimizing SPD Server resources. It includes hands-on practice with these tasks.
Prerequisites	Before attending this course, you should be able to • write SAS programs • understand the basics of your operating system.
Duration	3 days

SAS Intelligence Platform – Instructor-Based Training: Business Users

The courses in this path are intended for business users who will consume information from the data integration process for easy querying, reporting, and analysis.

Accessing SAS® from Microsoft Office Applications	Querying and Reporting Using SAS® Enterprise Guide®
Using SAS® Web Report Studio for Thin-Client Reporting	SAS® Enterprise Guide®: ANOVA, Regression, and Logistic Regression
Accessing Information Using the SAS® Information Delivery Portal	Advanced Querying Using SAS® Enterprise Guide®

■ Classroom
▨ Live Web

6

Accessing SAS® from Microsoft Office Applications

Audience

This Level I course is intended for Microsoft Office users with little or no programming experience who want to access the power of SAS directly from Microsoft Excel, Microsoft Word, and/or Microsoft PowerPoint. This course requires the SAS Intelligence Platform.

Course Description

This course provides an overview of the SAS Add-In for Microsoft Office and shows how it can be used to access SAS information directly from Microsoft Office applications. You learn how to run SAS Stored Processes and use SAS tasks for processing data directly from inside a Microsoft Excel spreadsheet, a Microsoft Word document, or a PowerPoint slide. In addition, you learn how to access and work with existing SAS data from Microsoft Excel.

Prerequisites

No SAS experience or programming experience is required although you should have some experience using Microsoft Office applications. Specifically, you should be able to

- open and save documents
- use the menus and toolbars to accomplish tasks
- navigate Word documents, PowerPoint presentations, and Excel spreadsheets.

Duration

1 day

Querying and Reporting Using SAS® Enterprise Guide®

Audience	This Level I course is designed for end users who are not programmers but who need to retrieve information from different sources, summarize it, and present it in tables and graphs.
Course Description	This course focuses on how to access, manage, summarize, and present data using SAS Enterprise Guide. The course teaches students how to navigate the menu-driven interface of SAS Enterprise Guide to accomplish tasks such as accessing local SAS and Microsoft Excel tables and remote relational databases; creating user-defined formats; managing, manipulating, and joining data using the SQL query builder; generating descriptive statistics, tabular summary reports, and ActiveX graphs; and automating and scheduling tasks. This course does not cover statistical analysis tasks.
Prerequisites	This course is designed for end users with no programming experience or SAS knowledge. Before attending this course, you should be familiar with Windows and other software, such as Microsoft Office or spreadsheet programs.
Duration	2 days (classroom) or 5 half-day sessions (Live Web)

Using SAS® Web Report Studio for Thin-Client Reporting

Audience	This Level I course is intended for anyone with little or no experience in other reporting tools or database technology. This course requires the SAS Intelligence Platform.
Course Description	This course provides an overview of SAS Web Report Studio. SAS Web Report Studio enables non-technical business users to find, interact with, create, and share reports based on corporate data. You learn how to navigate the SAS Web Report Studio interface and how to build simple and complex reports that surface information from tables, OLAP cubes, and SAS Stored Processes.
Prerequisites	No SAS experience or programming experience is required, although you should have some computer experience. Specifically, you should be able to • log on and off a computer • use a keyboard or mouse • use a Web browser to access information.
Duration	1 day

SAS® Enterprise Guide®: ANOVA, Regression, and Logistic Regression

Audience	This Level II course is designed for SAS Enterprise Guide users who want to perform statistical analyses using SAS Enterprise Guide software, a point-and-click interface to the SAS System.
Course Description	This course focuses on the following key areas: statistical inference, analysis of variance, multiple regression, categorical data analysis, and logistic regression. You learn to construct graphs to explore and summarize data, construct confidence intervals for means, test hypotheses, apply multiple comparison techniques in ANOVA, assess and correct collinearity in multiple regression, use diagnostic statistics to identify potential outliers in multiple regression, use chi-square statistics to detect associations among categorical variables, and fit a multiple logistic regression model.
Prerequisites	Before attending this course, you should • have completed an undergraduate course in statistics covering p-values, hypothesis testing, analysis of variance, and regression • be able to perform analyses and create data sets with SAS Enterprise Guide software. You can gain this experience by completing the Querying and Reporting Using SAS® Enterprise Guide® course.
Duration	3 days (classroom) or 5 half-day sessions (Live Web)

Accessing Information Using the SAS® Information Delivery Portal

Audience	This Level I course is for end users of the SAS Information Delivery Portal who want to customize their view of their organization's existing SAS Information Delivery Portal. This course requires the SAS Intelligence Platform.
Course Description	This course focuses on using the SAS Information Delivery Portal to view content developed in the SAS Business Intelligence environment. You learn how to navigate through the pages and portlets of the Portal. You learn how to add new pages and portlets to your view of the Portal, as well as how to add SAS Information Maps, SAS reports, and SAS Stored Processes to your Portal pages.
Prerequisites	No SAS experience or programming experience is required although you should have some computer experience. Specifically, you should be able to • log on and off a computer • use a keyboard or mouse • use a Web browser to access information.
Duration	1 day

Advanced Querying Using SAS® Enterprise Guide®

Audience
: This Level II course is intended for experienced SAS Enterprise Guide users who want to learn more about advanced querying techniques. Prior to attending the course, students should understand how to navigate the SAS Enterprise Guide environment, create projects, add data sources, accomplish basic analysis and reporting using tasks, and create queries. No SAS or SQL programming experience is required.

Course Description
: This course focuses on using the Query Builder within SAS Enterprise Guide, including manipulating character, numeric, and date values; converting variable type; and building conditional expressions using the Expression Builder. This course also addresses efficiency issues, such as joining tables and using a single query to group, summarize, and filter data.

Prerequisites
: Before attending this course, you should have taken the Querying and Reporting Using SAS® Enterprise Guide® course or completed the Getting Started Tutorial within SAS Enterprise Guide.

Duration
: 2 half-day sessions

SAS Intelligence Platform – Instructor-Based Training: IT Professionals

The courses in this path are intended for business analysts and IT professionals who will take the information from the data integration processing and make it easily consumable for the business users in the organization who need easy querying, reporting, and analysis.

| Creating, Distributing, and Using SAS® Stored Processes | Creating and Exploiting OLAP Using the SAS® System | Using SAS® Information Map Studio to Create Information Maps |

7

■ Classroom

Creating, Distributing, and Using SAS® Stored Processes

Audience	This Level III course is designed for programmers and analysts who want to understand, create, and exploit SAS Stored Processes. This course requires the SAS Intelligence Platform.
Course Description	This course defines SAS Stored Processes and demonstrates how to create and use them. In the course, SAS Enterprise Guide and the SAS windowing environment are used to create stored processes. The course also illustrates how SAS Stored Processes can be executed from the SAS Add-In for Microsoft Office, SAS Web Report Studio, and the SAS Information Delivery Portal.
Prerequisites	Familiarity with SAS programming is required. You can gain the necessary SAS knowledge by completing the SAS Programming I: Essentials course. To fully exploit the capabilities of stored processes, an understanding of the SAS macro language and SAS Enterprise Guide is helpful but not required. This knowledge can be acquired by completing the courses SAS® Macro Language and Querying and Reporting Using SAS® Enterprise Guide®, respectively.
Duration	2 days

Creating and Exploiting OLAP Using the SAS® System

Audience	This Level II course is designed for data modelers and system experts who want to understand, create, and exploit Online Analytical Processing (OLAP) using SAS. This course requires the SAS Intelligence Platform.
Course Description	This course defines SAS OLAP cubes and explores their characteristics. This course also demonstrates how to create and exploit SAS OLAP cubes using a variety of SAS products, including SAS OLAP Cube Studio, SAS Enterprise Guide, SAS Information Delivery Portal, SAS Web OLAP Viewer for Java, and Microsoft Excel with the SAS OLAP Data Provider.
Prerequisites	Familiarity with SAS programming and table structures is helpful but not required. You can gain SAS knowledge by completing the SAS® Programming I: Essentials course. Familiarity with Structured Query Language (SQL) or Multidimensional eXpressions (MDX) is also helpful, but not required.
Duration	2 days

Using SAS® Information Map Studio to Create Information Maps

Audience	This Level II course is for data modelers and data architects who have experience in data modeling, know the physical data, and have a strong understanding of the business domain. This course requires the SAS Intelligence Platform.
Course Description	This course provides an overview of SAS Information Map Studio. You learn how to navigate the SAS Information Map Studio interface, how to create information maps from simple to complex on single or multiple data sources, and how to create information maps on OLAP cubes. Additional topics include exporting and importing information maps as XML, using SAS Stored Processes with an information map, and using information maps in SAS Web Report Studio and the SAS Information Delivery Portal.
Prerequisites	A general understanding of Structured Query Language (SQL) and Multidimensional Expressions (MDX) is helpful but not required. You can gain the SQL knowledge by completing the SQL Processing with SAS course.
Duration	1 day

SAS Intelligence Platform – Instructor-Based Training: Application Developers

The courses in this path are intended for application developers who will incorporate the information from the data integration processing and make it easily consumable from customized applications.

NEW!

```
Developing Java Web
Applications Using
SAS® AppDev Studio™
Plug-ins
```

8   ■ Classroom

Developing Java Web Applications Using SAS® AppDev Studio™ Plug-ins

Audience	This Level III course is for experienced Java application developers who want to create Web applications using AppDev Studio 3.2 Eclipse Plug-ins.
Course Description	This course introduces a method for developing Web applications that use the power of server-side Java to generate dynamic content. Using the Eclipse development environment and the SAS AppDev Studio 3.2 Eclipse Plug-ins, you learn to build JavaServer Pages and servlet applications that instantly connect to SAS servers. After completing this course, you should be able to create a Web application that consists of JavaServer pages and servlets that access SAS data sources and the full analytic and computational capabilities of SAS software.
Prerequisites	Before attending this course, you should have knowledge of object-oriented programming as well as basic HTML and Java programming experience. Familiarity with the SAS Enterprise Intelligence Platform is helpful. You can gain the SAS knowledge by completing the Overview of SAS Business Intelligence and Data Integration Applications course. To be completely successful in this course, you should be able to perform the following tasks using the Java programming language:

- use primitive data types to store data within variables
- use operators, decision constructs, and loop constructs
- work with elements in an array
- create and initialize an object
- invoke a method on an object
- understand the use of import statements for library access

Duration	3 days

SAS Intelligence Platform – e-Learning

SAS Self-Paced
e-Learning

Convenient
Web-based training
available 24/7 when
and where you need it

Personalized
Select the specific
training you need

Interactive
Quizzes, guided practices,
simulations, and animation

http://support.sas.com/selfpaced

9

SAS Intelligence Platform – e-Learning

SAS e-Learning consists of the following components:

Tutorial	Free content that can be used to get new users of the product up and running as quickly as possible.
Lesson	1 to 2 hours of training in an easy-to-use browser-based interface with interactive questions and feedback.
Example	Provides an overview of a topic, step-by-step instructions for performing that topic, and an interpretation of the results.
Course	Collection of prebundled tutorials, lessons and/or examples.
Library	Collection of multiple courses.

10

SAS Intelligence Platform – e-Learning: Overview

☐ Overview

This **free** overview contains a series of in-depth demonstrations that describe the SAS business intelligence process, the roles people play in creating business intelligence, and the capabilities of each client application, and the underlying SAS Intelligence Platform architecture.

FREE!

SAS® Business
Intelligence Overview

11

SAS® Business Intelligence Overview

Description	This free overview contains a series of in-depth demonstrations that describe the SAS business intelligence process, the roles people play in creating business intelligence, and the capabilities of each client application, and the underlying SAS Intelligence Platform architecture.
Level of Difficulty	Beginner
Duration	Approximately 1 hour

SAS Intelligence Platform – e-Learning: Platform Administration Training

Library

This library is for information technology professionals who are responsible for administering the SAS®9 Intelligence Platform. This library covers both Service Pack 3 and Service Pack 4 updates to SAS 9.1.3.

SAS®9 Intelligence Platform Administration

12

SAS®9 Intelligence Platform Administration

Unit of Training	Library
Description	This library is for information technology professionals who are responsible for administering the SAS®9 Intelligence Platform 9.1.3 release. It covers both Service Pack 3 and Service Pack 4 updates. Before taking this e-learning course, you should have experience supporting operating systems and administering the user environment, although SAS experience is not required.
	The library prepares you to maintain, extend, and administer the SAS business intelligence system and addresses fundamentals of the architecture for the SAS Intelligence Platform, data access, and user maintenance.
Level of Difficulty	Advanced
Duration	Approximately 13 hours

SAS Intelligence Platform – e-Learning: Data Integration and ETL Training

Course
Lesson

This course provide training on the core concepts and processes associated with the data integration process.
The lesson provides training on using SAS Data Integration Studio.

An Introduction to Data Warehousing

Creating an ETL Process Flow Using SAS® Data Integration Studio

13

An Introduction to Data Warehousing

Unit of Training   Course

Description   This course uses a realistic case scenario to introduce you to the concepts and processes of data warehousing and to how you can use it to make intelligent and successful business decisions.

                        Although this course lays the foundation to the SAS data warehousing curriculum, it is not specific to SAS and does not use SAS software.

                        To get maximum benefit from this course, you should have a reasonable understanding of the concepts "transaction" and "operational data," and know basic database terminology. However, if these items are unfamiliar, you can still take the course because they are explained in a glossary.

Level of Difficulty   Beginner

Duration   Approximately 5 hours

Creating an ETL Process Flow Using SAS® Data Integration Studio

Unit of Training	Lesson
Description	SAS Data Integration Studio is a visual design tool that enables you to consolidate and manage enterprise data from a variety of source systems, applications, and technologies. Data can be managed and consolidated for traditional processes such as extracting, cleansing (data quality), transforming, and loading, or for other data integration purposes such as migration, synchronization, replication/promotion, and data management.

In this lesson, you learn how to use SAS Data Integration Studio to create an ETL process flow, which is a sequence of steps for the extraction, transformation, and loading of data. The lesson content covers Releases 3.3 and 3.4. |
| Level of Difficulty | Beginner |
| Duration | Approximately 2 hours |

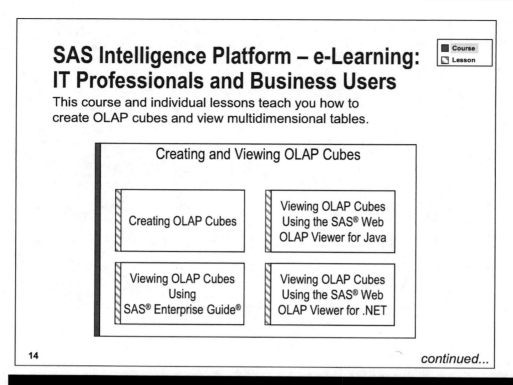

continued...

Creating and Viewing OLAP Cubes

Unit of Training	Course
Description	This course contains four lessons that provide at least 10 hours of training. Information architects will learn how to create a SAS OLAP cube, and using the OLAP viewer of their choice, information consumers will learn how to view cubes.
Level of Difficulty	Beginner
Duration	Approximately 10 hours

Creating OLAP Cubes

Unit of Training   Lesson

Description   An OLAP cube is a set of data that is organized and structured in a hierarchical, multidimensional arrangement, often with many dimensions and levels of data. The way that OLAP data is stored makes it readily available for detailed queries and analysis. The OLAP cube enables you or others to dynamically analyze data that has been summarized into multidimensional views and hierarchies. To create the cubes, you can use SAS OLAP Cube Studio, which is a Java interface.

This lesson guides you through the process of using SAS OLAP Cube Studio to define and create an OLAP cube.

Level of Difficulty   Beginner

Duration   Approximately 2 hours

Viewing OLAP Cubes Using SAS® Web OLAP Viewer for Java

Unit of Training   Lesson

Description   The SAS Web OLAP Viewer for Java is a Web application for analyzing the business information that is stored in OLAP data cubes. Using the viewer, you can navigate through multidimensional data by using drillable tables; add custom data items and summary data; filter and sort data; bookmark views; use conditional highlighting; and export data to Microsoft Excel.

Level of Difficulty   Beginner

Duration   Approximately 2.5 hours

Viewing OLAP Cubes Using SAS® Enterprise Guide®

Unit of Training   Lesson

Description   The OLAP Analyzer in SAS Enterprise Guide is an intuitive interface for analyzing the business information that is stored in OLAP data cubes. The OLAP Analyzer enables you to navigate through multidimensional data by using drillable graphs and tables, to add custom calculations, to run ad hoc queries, and to extract information for further analysis. Individual views can be saved with bookmarks, and slices of data can be used in other analytical procedures. In this lesson you will practice your new skills in a simulated SAS environment.

Level of Difficulty   Beginner

Duration   Approximately 2 hours

Viewing OLAP Cubes Using SAS® Web OLAP Viewer for .NET

Unit of Training	Lesson
Description	The SAS Web OLAP Viewer for .NET is an intuitive interface for analyzing the business information that is stored in OLAP data cubes. Using the viewer, you can navigate through multidimensional data by using drillable graphs and tables; add custom calculations; filter and sort data; bookmark views; and export data to Microsoft Excel.
Level of Difficulty	Beginner
Duration	Approximately 2 hours

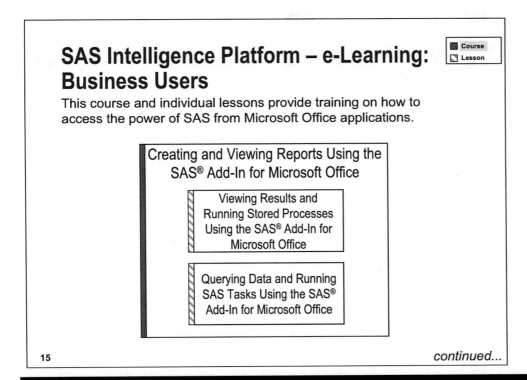

Creating and Viewing Reports Using the SAS® Add-In for Microsoft Office

Unit of Training	Course
Description	This course contains two lessons. The lessons contain interactive questions and quizzes, along with numerous opportunities to learn and practice in a simulated SAS environment.
	The SAS Add-In for Microsoft Office enables you to run sophisticated SAS analyses on large SAS data sources while working in the familiar Microsoft Office environment. In these lessons you learn how to use the SAS add-in to view and refresh SAS results in Microsoft Office files. You also learn to open and query a large SAS data source, to analyze your data by running stored processes (predefined SAS analyses) and SAS tasks, and to create both results and (in Excel only) output data sets.
Level of Difficulty	Beginner
Duration	Approximately 6 hours

Viewing Results and Running Stored Processes Using the SAS® Add-In for Microsoft Office

Unit of Training	Lesson
Description	The SAS Add-In for Microsoft Office enables you to run sophisticated SAS analyses on large SAS data sources while working in the familiar environment of Microsoft Office. Results are embedded in Microsoft Word documents and Microsoft Excel spreadsheets. In this lesson, you learn to use the SAS add-in to view results in existing Microsoft Office reports, and to run predefined SAS analyses called stored processes.
Level of Difficulty	Beginner
Duration	Approximately 2 hours

Querying Data and Running SAS Tasks Using the SAS® Add-In for Microsoft Office

Unit of Training	Lesson
Description	Using the SAS Add-in for Microsoft Office, you can work with large SAS data sources in the familiar environment of Microsoft Office. In this lesson, you learn to use the SAS add-in to open and query a SAS data source, to analyze your data by using SAS tasks, and to create results in Microsoft Office files. You also learn to create an output data set in an Excel workbook.
Level of Difficulty	Beginner
Duration	Approximately 3 hours

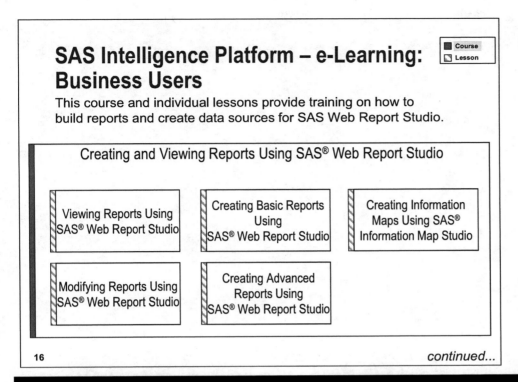

continued...

Creating and Viewing Reports Using SAS® Web Report Studio

Unit of Training	Course
Description	This course contains five lessons that provide at least 15 hours of instruction. In these lessons, information architects learn how to create information maps. Information consumers learn how to create, modify, and view basic and advanced reports.
Level of Difficulty	Beginner
Duration	Approximately 15 hours

Viewing Reports Using SAS® Web Report Studio

Unit of Training	Lesson
Description	SAS Web Report Studio is a Web application that enables you to view reports and modify reports that contain information about your business. In this lesson, you learn to use SAS Web Report Studio to view saved reports and stored processes, to create quick reports, to perform simple modifications to reports, to save reports, and to export the data from a report.
Level of Difficulty	Beginner
Duration	Approximately 2 hours

Creating Basic Reports Using SAS® Web Report Studio

Unit of Training	Lesson
Description	SAS Web Report Studio enables you to create both basic and advanced reports quickly and easily. Creating reports does not require you to know how to program or to understand database complexity.
	In this lesson, you learn to create basic reports by using the Report Wizard and report templates. You also learn to edit a basic report by using the Edit Report view. The basic reports that you create in this lesson are based on a single, relational data source; have one section; and contain a limited number of the report elements and features that are available in SAS Web Report Studio. Creating advanced reports and reports based on multidimensional data sources by using SAS Web Report Studio is covered in later lessons.
Level of Difficulty	Beginner
Duration	Approximately 3 hours

Creating Information Maps Using SAS® Information Map Studio

Unit of Training	Lesson
Description	In organizations today, business users need to create reports from business data in order to make intelligent and timely business decisions. In many situations, the IT group cannot fulfill business users' frequent requests for reports. However, the business users who consume information might not be trained to understand and interpret the complex data warehouses, where data is stored. SAS Information Map Studio enables information architects and query designers who are skilled in interpreting complex data structures to bridge the gap between the data warehouse and the business user who views or builds reports from the data.
	An information map hides the details of the physical data view from the business users, while allowing business users access to the most current data needed for business reporting. Information maps are required for creating reports using SAS Web Report Studio. In this lesson you learn how to create and enhance information maps.
Level of Difficulty	Beginner
Duration	Approximately 2.5 hours

Modifying Reports Using SAS® Web Report Studio

Unit of Training	Lesson
Description	SAS Web Report Studio enables you to modify your existing reports with a variety of tools. These tools enable you to modify your reports by changing how data is arranged, by changing what data is displayed, and by changing how data is presented in tables and graphs. This lesson focuses on the tasks for modifying reports using SAS Web Report Studio. These tasks include rearranging, sorting, filtering, ranking, and highlighting your data in addition to adding totals and subtotals to your reports. Other lessons for SAS Web Report Studio address creating basic and advanced reports.
Level of Difficulty	Beginner
Duration	Approximately 3.5 hours

Creating Advanced Reports Using SAS® Web Report Studio

Unit of Training	Lesson
Description	Using the Edit Report view, you can access the full range of query and report features that SAS Web Report Studio offers. Many of the features that are available in the Edit Report view are not available in the Report Wizard. In this lesson, you learn to create reports that have advanced features, to schedule reports, and to create and manage report templates.
Level of Difficulty	Advanced
Duration	Approximately 3.5 hours

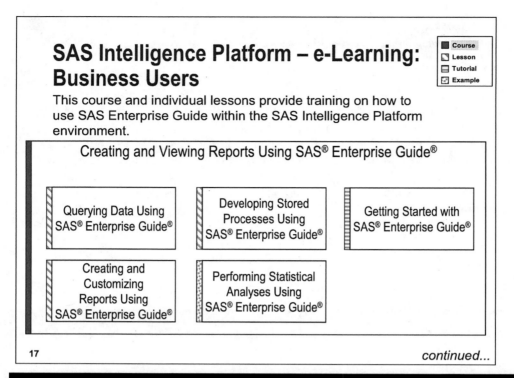

Creating and Viewing Reports Using SAS® Enterprise Guide®

Unit of Training	Course
Description	This course contains a Getting Started tutorial and four lessons that provide over 10 hours of training. The content of these lessons ranges from learning how to use SAS Enterprise Guide for creating basic reports and queries to learning how to develop stored processes. Note that in order to develop and run stored processes, you must have the SAS®9 Intelligence Platform installed at your site.
Level of Difficulty	Beginner
Duration	Approximately 10.5 hours

Querying Data Using SAS® Enterprise Guide®

Unit of Training	Lesson
Description	To help you answer questions about your data, you can use SAS Enterprise Guide to create, run, and save queries (requests to retrieve data). Using queries, you can examine relationships between data values; subset and sort your data; compute values quickly; join tables to combine data from different sources; and group and summarize data. Depending on your needs, you can create tables or reports from your queries, and you can store queries for future use. With SAS Enterprise Guide, you do not need to know any programming statements to produce a variety of basic and advanced queries. This lesson guides you through creating several queries of increasing complexity. After you create queries, you can use them to run SAS Enterprise Guide tasks.
	This lesson enables you to select the version of SAS Enterprise Guide software you are using. The content of the lesson will change to correspond to your selected version. The SAS Enterprise Guide 4.1 version of the lesson enables you to practice in a simulated SAS environment and requires you to have the latest version of Macromedia Flash Player installed. The SAS Enterprise Guide 2.0 and 3.0 lessons require you to have the corresponding version of SAS Enterprise Guide software installed, in order to do the practices. You can also substitute SAS Learning Edition 2.0 for SAS Enterprise Guide 2.0 software.
Level of Difficulty	Beginner
Duration	Approximately 1.5 hours

Developing Stored Processes Using SAS® Enterprise Guide®

Unit of Training	Lesson
Description	SAS Stored Processes are SAS programs that are stored and executed on a central server and described by metadata. Stored processes offer benefits over traditional SAS programs in accessibility, manageability, security, and reusability. In this lesson, you learn to create, register, and execute stored processes by using SAS Enterprise Guide. You learn to create stored processes from SAS tasks and from SAS code. You learn the benefits of using parameters with your stored processes and how to create them. Finally, you learn how to update existing stored processes and how to create an HTML-based interface to a stored process.
Level of Difficulty	Beginner
Duration	Approximately 3 hours

Getting Started with SAS® Enterprise Guide®

Unit of Training	Tutorial
Description	In this step-by-step tutorial, you learn to do basic tasks in SAS Enterprise Guide: create a project, add data to a project, and run tasks to analyze and report on your data. You learn how to run tasks that create a listing report and a bar chart, and to use a query to modify data for reports.
	The tutorial is designed to be used in conjunction with SAS Enterprise Guide software. To get the most out of this tutorial, you should have SAS Enterprise Guide software running along with a browser that displays the tutorial.
Level of Difficulty	Beginner
Duration	Approximately 2 hours

Creating and Customizing Reports Using SAS® Enterprise Guide®

Unit of Training	Lesson
Description	SAS Enterprise Guide is not only for point-and-click users! You can use the software to write and submit SAS programs, access data, and keep your programs, output, and logs organized in a project. You can even allow the point-and-click interface to do some of your programming work and then edit the SAS program that is generated. In this lesson you learn to use SAS Enterprise Guide to write and submit your own code. You also learn how to generate and edit code from point-and-click tasks and queries. For this lesson, you should have some experience with SAS programming, but no SAS Enterprise Guide experience is necessary.
	This lesson enables you to select the version of SAS Enterprise Guide software that you are using. The content of the lesson will change to correspond to your selected version. The SAS Enterprise Guide 4.1 version of the lesson enables you to practice in a simulated SAS environment and requires you to have the latest version of Macromedia Flash Player installed. The SAS Enterprise Guide 2.0 and 3.0 lessons require you to have the corresponding version of SAS Enterprise Guide software installed in order to do the practices. You can also substitute SAS Learning Edition 2.0 for SAS Enterprise Guide 2.0 software.
Level of Difficulty	Beginner
Duration	Approximately 2 hours

Performing Statistical Analyses Using SAS® Enterprise Guide®

Unit of Training	Example
Description	SAS Enterprise Guide has many statistical analysis tasks that you can run against your data without any SAS programming knowledge. Using SAS Enterprise Guide, you can run tasks that generate descriptive statistics, explore distributions to test hypotheses, compare means and analyze experiments, analyze for K independent variables, and generate control charts for various types of data. These are only a few of the many statistical analyses that you can perform using this software.

This product is a collection of examples that you can use to learn how to run statistical analyses in SAS Enterprise Guide. It is assumed that you are already familiar with statistics and statistics terminology. Each example includes an overview of the statistical analysis, step-by-step instructions for running the task in SAS Enterprise Guide, and an interpretation of the results. Working through these examples will help you become familiar with using SAS Enterprise Guide for statistical analysis.

This lesson enables you to select the version of SAS Enterprise Guide software you are using. The content of the lesson will change to correspond to your selected version. The SAS Enterprise Guide 4.1 version of the lesson enables you to practice in a simulated SAS environment and requires you to have the latest version of Macromedia Flash Player installed. The SAS Enterprise Guide 2.0 and 3.0 lessons require you to have the corresponding version of SAS Enterprise Guide software installed in order to do the practices. You can also substitute SAS Learning Edition 2.0 for SAS Enterprise Guide 2.0 software.

Level of Difficulty	Beginner
Duration	Approximately 2 hours

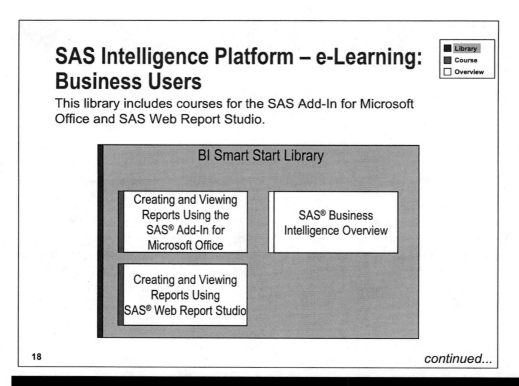

SAS Intelligence Platform – e-Learning: Business Users

This library includes courses for the SAS Add-In for Microsoft Office and SAS Web Report Studio.

BI Smart Start Library

Creating and Viewing Reports Using the SAS® Add-In for Microsoft Office

SAS® Business Intelligence Overview

Creating and Viewing Reports Using SAS® Web Report Studio

18   *continued...*

BI Smart Start Library

Unit of Training	Library
Description	This library includes a BI Overview containing 12 five-minute movie segments that describe the SAS business intelligence process, the roles people play in creating business intelligence, and the capabilities of each client tool. This Overview provides you with a solid background before taking the how to lessons.
	There are seven lessons in the library and each lesson is approximately three hours in length. The lessons contain interactive questions and quizzes, along with numerous opportunities to learn and practice in a simulated SAS environment.
	These lessons teach information architects how to create information maps using SAS Information Map Studio. Information maps are required in order to create and view reports using SAS Web Report Studio. These lessons teach information consumers how to easily create and view basic and advanced reports using SAS Web Report Studio. Information consumers also learn how to use the SAS Add-In for Microsoft Office to work with SAS data, run SAS analyses, and create both results and output data sets in the Microsoft Office environment.
Level of Difficulty	Beginner
Duration	Approximately 20.5 hours

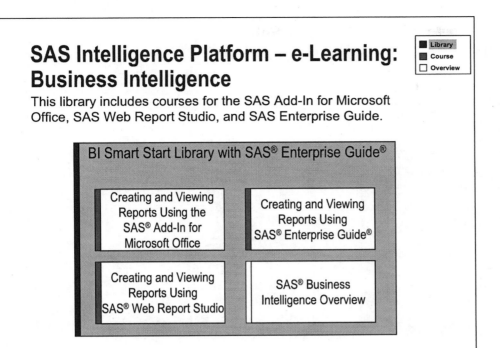

BI Smart Start with SAS® Enterprise Guide®

Unit of Training	Library
Description	This library contains the BI Overview and all lessons within the BI Smart Start Library, plus the SAS Enterprise Guide course. The library also contains instruction for multiple versions of the software products covered. When you enter the library, you can select which version of the software product that you have at your site and the content of the lesson changes to correspond with your software.

The SAS Enterprise Guide course contains a Getting Started tutorial and four lessons that provide at least 11 more hours of training. The content of these lessons ranges from learning how to use SAS Enterprise Guide for creating basic reports and queries to learning how to develop stored processes. |
| Level of Difficulty | Beginner |
| Duration | Approximately 31 hours |

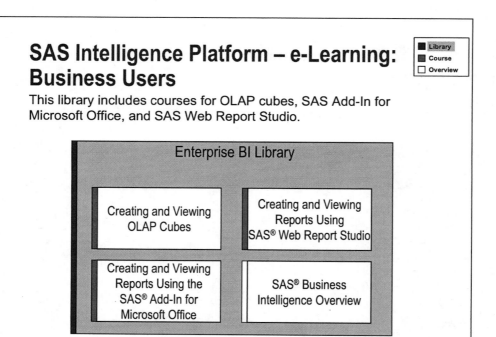

continued...

Enterprise BI Library

Unit of Training	Library
Description	This library includes a BI Overview containing 12 five-minute movie segments that describe the SAS business intelligence process, the roles that people play in creating business intelligence, and the capabilities of each client tool. This Overview provides you with a solid background before taking the how-to lessons.
	There are 10 lessons in the library and each lesson is approximately three hours in length. The lessons contain interactive questions and quizzes, along with numerous opportunities to learn and practice in a simulated SAS environment.
	In these lessons, information architects learn how to create OLAP cubes using SAS OLAP Cube Studio and information maps using SAS Information Map Studio.
	Information consumers learn how to use SAS Web Report Studio to create, modify, and view basic and advanced reports, including multidimensional reports. They also learn how to use the SAS Add-In for Microsoft Office to work with SAS data, run SAS analyses, and create both results and output data sets in the Microsoft Office environment. In addition, information consumers learn to view OLAP cubes using the OLAP viewer of their choice.
Level of Difficulty	Beginner
Duration	Approximately 26 hours

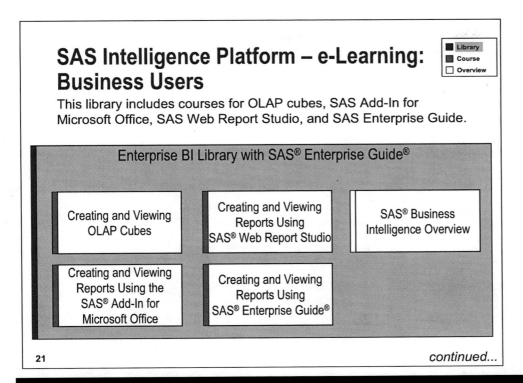

21   continued...

Enterprise BI Library with SAS® Enterprise Guide®

Unit of Training	Library
Description	This library contains the BI Overview and all 10 lessons within the Enterprise BI Library, plus the SAS Enterprise Guide course. The library also contains instruction covering multiple versions of each software product. When you enter a course within the library, you are able to select the version of the software you have and the content of the course changes to correspond with your software version.
	The SAS Enterprise Guide course contains a Getting Started tutorial and five lessons that provide at least 13 additional hours of training. The content of these SAS Enterprise Guide lessons ranges from learning how to use SAS Enterprise Guide for creating basic reports and queries to learning how to develop stored processes.
Level of Difficulty	Beginner
Duration	Approximately 46.5 hours

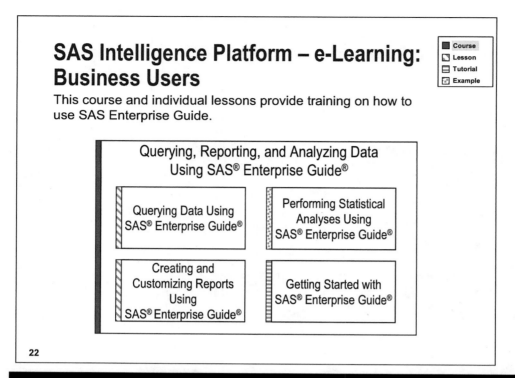

Querying, Reporting, and Analyzing Data Using SAS® Enterprise Guide®

Unit of Training   Course

Description   SAS Enterprise Guide is an intuitive point-and-click interface that enables you to
                        quickly and efficiently access, manage, analyze, and present your data without
                        knowing any SAS programming.

Level of Difficulty   Beginner

Duration   Approximately 8 hours

Querying Data Using SAS® Enterprise Guide®

Unit of Training   Lesson

Description   To help you answer questions about your data, you can use SAS Enterprise Guide to create, run, and save queries (requests to retrieve data). Using queries, you can examine relationships between data values; subset and sort your data; compute values quickly; join tables to combine data from different sources; and group and summarize data. Depending on your needs, you can create tables or reports from your queries, and you can store queries for future use. With SAS Enterprise Guide, you do not need to know any programming statements to produce a variety of basic and advanced queries. This lesson guides you through creating several queries of increasing complexity. After you create queries, you can use them to run SAS Enterprise Guide tasks.

This lesson enables you to select the version of SAS Enterprise Guide software that you are using. The content of the lesson will change to correspond to your selected version. The SAS Enterprise Guide 4.1 version of the lesson enables you to practice in a simulated SAS environment and requires you to have the latest version of Macromedia Flash Player installed. The SAS Enterprise Guide 2.0 and 3.0 lessons require you to have the corresponding version of SAS Enterprise Guide software installed in order to do the practices. You can also substitute SAS Learning Edition 2.0 for SAS Enterprise Guide 2.0 software.

Level of Difficulty   Beginner

Duration   Approximately 1.5 hours

Performing Statistical Analyses Using SAS® Enterprise Guide®

Unit of Training	Example
Description	SAS Enterprise Guide has many statistical analysis tasks that you can run against your data without any SAS programming knowledge. Using SAS Enterprise Guide, you can run tasks that generate descriptive statistics, explore distributions to test hypotheses, compare means and analyze experiments, analyze for K independent variables, and generate control charts for various types of data. These are only a few of the many statistical analyses that you can perform using this software.
	This product is a collection of examples that you can use to learn how to run statistical analyses in SAS Enterprise Guide. It is assumed that you are already familiar with statistics and statistics terminology. Each example includes an overview of the statistical analysis, step-by-step instructions for running the task in SAS Enterprise Guide, and an interpretation of the results. Working through these examples will help you become familiar with using SAS Enterprise Guide for statistical analysis.
	This lesson enables you to select the version of SAS Enterprise Guide software that you are using. The content of the lesson will change to correspond to your selected version. The SAS Enterprise Guide 4.1 version of the lesson enables you to practice in a simulated SAS environment and requires you to have the latest version of Macromedia Flash Player installed. The SAS Enterprise Guide 2.0 and 3.0 lessons require you to have the corresponding version of SAS Enterprise Guide software installed in order to do the practices. You can also substitute SAS Learning Edition 2.0 for SAS Enterprise Guide 2.0 software.
Level of Difficulty	Beginner
Duration	Approximately 2 hours

Creating and Customizing Reports Using SAS® Enterprise Guide®

Unit of Training	Lesson
Description	SAS Enterprise Guide is not only for point-and-click users! You can use the software to write and submit SAS programs, access data, and keep your programs, output, and logs organized in a project. You can even allow the point-and-click interface to do some of your programming work, and then edit the SAS program that is generated. In this lesson you learn to use SAS Enterprise Guide to write and submit your own code. You also learn how to generate and edit code from point-and-click tasks and queries. For this lesson, you should have some experience with SAS programming, but no SAS Enterprise Guide experience is necessary.

This lesson enables you to select the version of SAS Enterprise Guide software that you are using. The content of the lesson will change to correspond to your selected version. The SAS Enterprise Guide 4.1 version of the lesson enables you to practice in a simulated SAS environment and requires you to have the latest version of Macromedia Flash Player installed. The SAS Enterprise Guide 2.0 and 3.0 lessons require you to have the corresponding version of SAS Enterprise Guide software installed in order to do the practices. You can also substitute SAS Learning Edition 2.0 for SAS Enterprise Guide 2.0 software.

Level of Difficulty	Beginner
Duration	Approximately 2 hours

Getting Started with SAS® Enterprise Guide®

Unit of Training	Tutorial
Description	In this step-by-step tutorial you learn to do basic tasks in SAS Enterprise Guide: create a project, add data to a project, and run tasks to analyze and report on your data. You learn how to run tasks that create a listing report and a bar chart, and to use a query to modify data for reports.

The tutorial is designed to be used in conjunction with SAS Enterprise Guide software. To get the most out of this tutorial, you should have SAS Enterprise Guide software running along with a browser displaying the tutorial.

Level of Difficulty	Beginner
Duration	Approximately 2 hours

SAS Intelligence Platform Training

Appendix B Administrative Topics

B.1 Registering a Stored Process for Use in SAS Web Report Studio

Objectives

- Introduce the SAS Management Console.
- Learn how to make stored processes available to SAS Web Report Studio.

3

What Is the SAS Management Console?

The SAS Management Console provides a single interface for many administrative tasks for the SAS System. Specific administrative tasks are supported by plug-ins to the SAS Management Console.

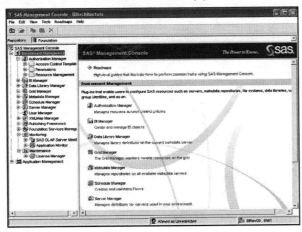

4

SAS Management Console

The BI Manager plug-in in the SAS Management Console can be used to register information for use in SAS Web Report Studio.

You must have WriteMetadata privileges to use the BI Manager in the SAS Management Console.

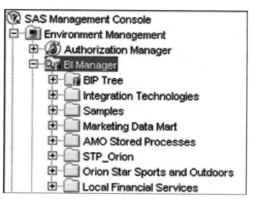

5

Stored Processes and SAS Web Report Studio

A stored process can be included in a report. To add a stored process to your report, you must be in the Edit Report view. Select the Insert Stored Process object in the report grid.

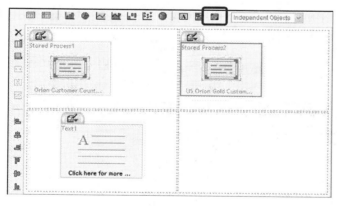

6

Importing a Stored Processes

In order for a stored process to be available in SAS Web Report Studio, it must be registered in a specific location using the BI Manager plug-in:

BIP Tree ⇨ **ReportStudio** ⇨ **Shared** ⇨ **Reports** ⇨ **StoredProcesses**

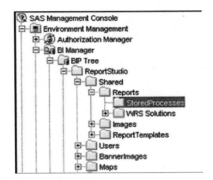

7

Registering a Stored Process

To register a stored process in the location necessary to be used with SAS Web Report Studio, copy the stored process from its original location.

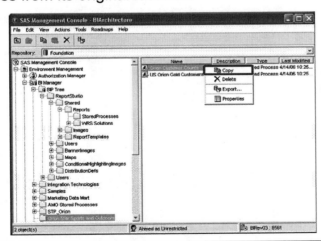

8

Registering a Stored Process

Paste the stored process into the following location:

BI Manager ⇨ **BIP Tree** ⇨ **ReportStudio** ⇨ **Shared** ⇨ **Reports** ⇨ **StoredProcesses**

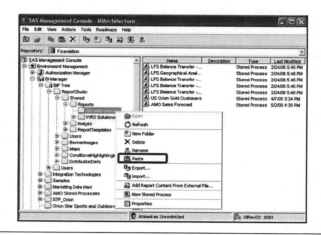

9

B.2 Registering Banner Images for Use in SAS Web Report Studio

Objectives

- Learn how to make banner images available to SAS Web Report Studio.

11

Banner Images

SAS Web Report Studio allows the use of banner images in both the report header and the report footer.

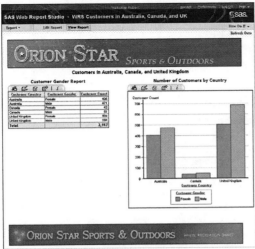

12

Banner Images

Banner images can be defined to the SAS Web Report Studio environment by an administrator.

Administrators use SAS Management Console's BI Manager plug-in to import banner images and set their metadata properties.

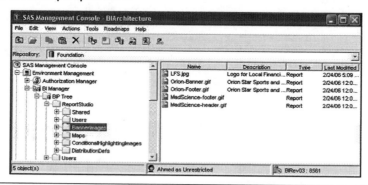

13

Importing a Banner Image

Banner images need to be imported into a specific location in the BI Manager:

BIP Tree ⇨ ReportStudio ⇨ BannerImages

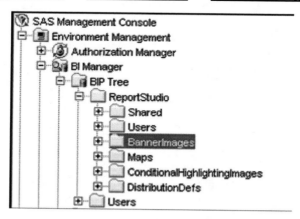

14

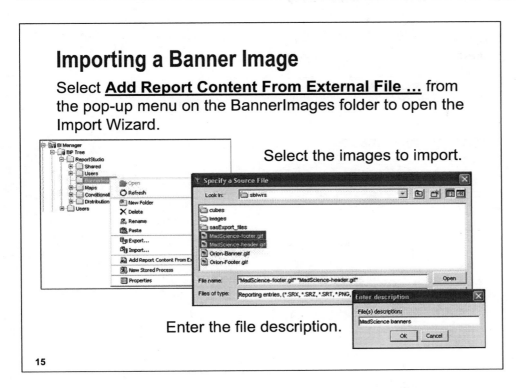

Importing a Banner Image

Select **Add Report Content From External File ...** from the pop-up menu on the BannerImages folder to open the Import Wizard.

Select the images to import.

Enter the file description.

15

✎ You can also import banner images that have been saved as an export package file (.spk) by selecting **Import ...**.

B.3 Registering Images for Use in SAS Web Report Studio

Objectives

- Learn how to make graphic images available to SAS Web Report Studio.

17

Image Objects

SAS Web Report Studio allows Image objects to be added to the body of a report.

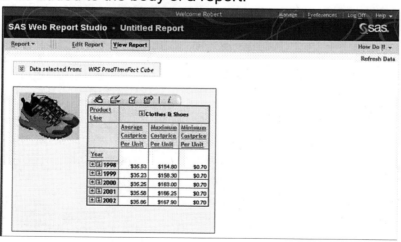

18

Importing Images

Images can be imported into to the SAS Web Report Studio environment by an administrator using SAS Management Console's BI Manager plug-in.

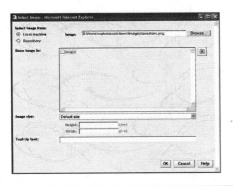

Report authors can also import images directly in SAS Web Report Studio using the Select Image window when editing the properties for the image in the Edit Report view.

19

Importing Images

Images need to be imported into a specific location in the BI Manager:

BIP Tree ⇨ ReportStudio ⇨ Shared ⇨ Images

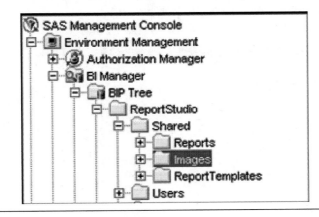

20

Images can also be stored in a user area. Storing images in the shared location makes them available to all people using SAS Web Report Studio, based on security.

Importing Images

Select **Add Report Content From External File ...** from the pop-up menu on the Images folder to open the Import Wizard.

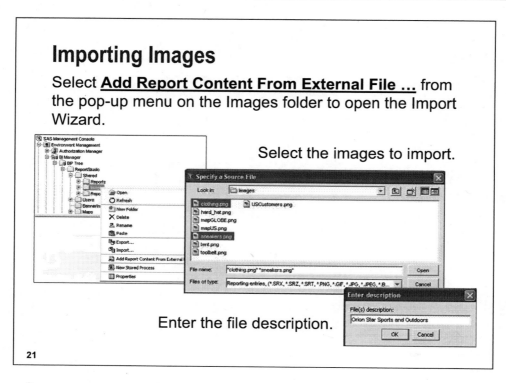

Select the images to import.

Enter the file description.

21

✎ You can also import images that have been saved as an export package file (.spk) by selecting **Import ...**.

Importing Images

Images can also be added directly from SAS Web Report Studio's Edit Report view. In the Select Image window, select **Local machine**, browse for the image, and select it. The image will be used in the report and also saved in the repository.

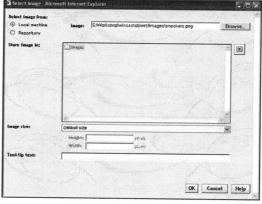

22

Appendix C Index